SPECTRUM

Grade 4

Common Core
Language Arts and Math

Published by Spectrum®
An imprint of Carson-Dellosa Publishing LLC
Greensboro, North Carolina

Spectrum®
An imprint of Carson-Dellosa Publishing LLC
P.O. Box 35665
Greensboro, NC 27425 USA

ISBN 978-1-4838-0452-1

01-031141151

© Carson-Dellosa • CD-704504

Table of Contents

Introduction to the Common Core State Standards: Grade 4 4

How to Use This Book. 5

Grade 4 Common Core State Standards: English Language Arts Overview. 6–9

Language Arts Practice Pages 10–63

Making Inferences • Themes • Characters, Settings, and Events • Compare and Contrast • Context Clues • Reading Poetry • Point of View • Main Idea • Main Idea and Details • Visual Aids in Text • Making a Chart • Words in Text • Reading a Chart • Reading a Time Line • Reading in Content Areas • Firsthand and Secondhand Accounts • Cause and Effect • Writing an Opinion • Examples and Details • Writing to Inform • Revising and Editing • Writing to Inform • Writing Directions • Sensory Words • Writing Dialogue • Writing a Story Ending • Writing a Story • The Writing Process • Relative Pronouns and Adverbs • Verb Tenses • Complete Sentences • Adjectives, Prepositional Phrases, and Homophones • Capitalization and Punctuation • Using Quotation Marks • Spelling • Word Choice • Ending Punctuation • Word Parts • Similes and Metaphors • Idioms • Figurative Language • Synonyms and Antonyms • Word Meanings

Grade 4 Common Core State Standards: Math Overview. 64–67

Math Practice Pages 68–121

Understanding Multiplication • Word Problems • Multi-Step Problems • Factors and Multiples • Patterns • Place Value • Comparing Numbers • Rounding Multi-Digit Numbers • Addition and Subtraction • Multiplication • Division • Equivalent Fractions • Comparing Fractions • Adding and Subtracting Fractions • Mixed Numbers • Adding Mixed Numbers • Subtracting Mixed Numbers • Multiplying Whole Numbers and Fractions • Decimals: Tenths • Decimals: Hundredths • Decimal Notation • Ordering Decimals • Comparing Decimals • Converting Measurements • Word Problems: Time • Word Problems: Money • Perimeter • Area • Line Plots • Understanding Angles • Measuring Angles • Adding Angle Measurements • Types of Lines • Parallel and Perpendicular Lines • Triangles • Symmetry

Answer Key 122

Introduction to the Common Core State Standards
Grade 4

Why Are Common Core State Standards Important for My Child?

The Common Core State Standards are a set of guidelines that outline what children are expected to learn at school. Most U.S. states have voluntarily adopted the standards. Teachers, principals, and administrators in these states use the standards as a blueprint for classroom lessons, district curriculum, and statewide tests. The standards were developed by a state-led collaboration between the Council of Chief State School Officers (CCSSO) and the National Governors Association (NGA).

The Common Core Standards set high expectations for your child's learning. They are up-to-date with 21st century technology and draw on the best practices of excellent schools around the world. They focus on important skills in reading, language arts, and math. Common Core State Standards aim to ensure that your child will be college and career ready by the end of high school and able to compete in our global world.

What Are the Common Core State Standards for My Fourth Grade Student?

Common Core State Standards for your fourth grader are designed to build a solid foundation for reading, literacy, and mathematical understanding. On practice pages in this book, you will find references to specific Common Core Standards that teachers will expect your child to know by the end of the year. Completing activities on these pages will help your child master essential skills for success in fourth grade.

A Sample of Common Core Language Arts Skills for Grade 4

- Make inferences, or educated guesses, based on reading.
- Explain differences between poems, drama, and prose writing.
- Learn about problem/solution, cause/effect, and other ways to organize ideas logically.
- Read information presented in charts, graphs, and time lines.
- Write to give an opinion, share information, and tell stories.
- Understand and use prepositional phrases.
- Use commas and quotation marks correctly to write dialogue.

A Sample of Common Core Math Skills for Grade 4

- Solve multi-step word problems involving addition, subtraction, multiplication, and division.
- Work with number patterns.
- Compare two fractions to tell which is greater or less.
- Multiply fractions.
- Change fractions to decimals and decimals to fractions.
- Find the perimeter and area of rectangular shapes.
- Measure angles in degrees.

© Copyright 2010. National Governors Association Center for Best Practices and Council of Chief State School Officers. All rights reserved.

How to Use This Book

In this book, you will find a complete **Common Core State Standards Overview** for fourth grade English Language Arts (pages 6–9) and Math (pages 64–67). Read these pages to learn more about the Common Core Standards and what you can expect your child to learn at school this year.

Then, choose **Practice Pages** that best address your child's needs for building skills that meet specific standards. Help your child complete practice pages and check the answers.

At the bottom of each practice page, you will find a **Helping at Home** tip that provides fun and creative ideas for additional practice with the skill at home.

Common Core State Standards for English Language Arts*

The following parent-friendly explanations of fourth grade Common Core English language arts standards are provided to help you understand what your child will learn in school this year. Practice pages listed will help your child master each skill.

Complete Common Core State Standards may be found here: www.corestandards.org.

RL/RI.4 Reading Standards for Literature and Informational Text

Key Ideas and Details
(Standards: RL.4.1, RL.4.2, RL.4.3, RI.4.1, RI.4.2, RI.4.3)

Your child will answer questions about details and examples used in texts. He or she will explain what the text says directly and make inferences, or educated guesses, about what is not directly stated. • **Practice pages:** 10, 12, 13, 16, 18, 19, 21–26, 28–31, 44

Your child will summarize texts and describe their themes or main ideas.
• **Practice pages:** 11, 21

Your child will think about characters, settings, and events from stories. For example, he or she will describe a character's thoughts, words, and actions and explain what they say about that character. • **Practice pages:** 10, 12–16, 20

Your child will read about history, science, and technology and explain procedures, events, and ideas described in nonfiction articles. • **Practice pages:** 21–27, 30, 31

Craft and Structure
(Standards: RL.4.4, RL.4.5, RL.4.6, RI.4.4, RI.4.5, RI.4.6)

Your child will determine the meanings of words and phrases found in texts.
• **Practice pages:** 17, 22–25, 27, 30, 31, 57

Your child will read stories, plays, and poems and discuss the differences between them.
• **Practice pages:** 18, 19

Your child will think about whether ideas in an article are organized by time, cause/effect, compare/contrast, problem/solution, or another strategy. • **Practice pages:** 28, 29, 34

Your child will think about point of view and determine who is telling a story. He or she will compare stories told by first-person and third-person narrators. • **Practice pages:** 14, 15, 20

Your child will compare firsthand and secondhand accounts of the same event or topic.
• **Practice pages: 32, 33**

Integration of Knowledge and Skills
(Standards: RL.4.7, RL.4.9, RI.4.7, RI.4.8, RI.4.9)

Your child will make connections between a text and a visual presentation of the text. For example, your child will compare a story's text to its illustrations or to a movie version of the story. • **Practice pages: 12, 13**

Your child will read and understand information presented in charts, graphs, diagrams, time lines, etc. • **Practice pages: 24–26, 28, 29**

Your child will explain how an author uses reasons and evidence to back up his or her points.
• **Practice page: 21**

Your child will compare and contrast stories that have similar themes or compare and contrast similar stories from different cultures. • **Practice pages: 14, 15**

Your child will combine information from two different texts in order to speak or write knowledgeably about a topic. • **Practice pages: 32, 33, 35**

W.4 Writing Standards

Text Types and Purposes
(Standards: W.4.1, W.4.2, W.4.3)

Your child will state an opinion in writing, giving reasons and information to support the opinion. • **Practice pages: 36, 37**

Your child will write to provide facts and information about a topic.
• **Practice pages: 35, 38, 39, 41, 42**

Your child will write stories with descriptive details and clear sequences of events.
• **Practice pages: 43–46**

Production and Distribution of Writing
(Standards: W.4.5, W.4.6)

Your child will revise and edit writing to make sure it is correct, to make it more interesting, and to answer questions from readers. • **Practice pages: 40, 47**

Common Core State Standards for English Language Arts*

Your child will use technology, including the Internet, to produce and publish writing. He or she will learn keyboarding skills. • **Practice pages: 40, 47**

Research to Build and Present Knowledge
(Standard: W.4.7)

Your child will gather ideas for writing by using a variety of sources to conduct research.
• **Practice pages: 32, 33, 39, 41**

L.4 Language Standards

Conventions of Standard English
(Standards: L.4.1a, L.4.1b, L.4.1c, L.4.1d, L.4.1e, L.4.1f, L.4.1g, L.4.2a, L.4.2b, L.4.2c, L.4.2d)

Your child will learn to use relative, or non-specific, pronouns such as who and which and relative adverbs such as when and where. • **Practice page: 48**

Your child will use the progressive verb tense (example: I am walking) to indicate an action that is ongoing. • **Practice page: 49**

Your child will learn to use modal auxiliary verbs such as may and must to show mood or likelihood. • **Practice page: 49**

Your child will learn which adjectives should come first in a list of adjectives (example: little red bag, not red little bag). • **Practice page: 51**

Your child will learn to form prepositional phrases such as above the desk and for my friend.
• **Practice page: 51**

Your child will write complete sentences that include a subject and verb (example: I went home) and avoid sentence fragments (example: Went home) and run-on sentences (I went home she did, too). • **Practice page: 50**

Your child will learn the correct use of homophones (words that sound alike but have different spellings and meanings) and other words that are frequently confused (examples: to, too, two). • **Practice pages: 18, 19, 51**

Your child will use correct capitalization and punctuation. He or she will learn to use commas and quotation marks correctly when writing dialogue (example: He said, "Come here!").
• **Practice pages: 44, 52, 53**

Your child will check spelling carefully, using a dictionary when needed to look up the spellings of words. • **Practice page: 54**

Knowledge of Language
(Standards: L.4.3a, L.4.3b, L.4.3c)

Your child will choose words, phrases, and punctuation to convey ideas and feelings precisely. • **Practice pages: 55, 56**

Your child will think about times when informal language is OK and when more formal language is required. • **Practice page: 55**

Vocabulary Acquisition and Use
(Standards: L.4.4a, L.4.4b, L.4.5a, L.4.5b, L.4.5c, L.4.6)

Your child will search the surrounding text for context clues to the meaning of an unknown word. • **Practice pages: 17, 27, 57**

Your child will study prefixes, suffixes, and word roots from Greek and Latin. • **Practice page: 58**

Your child will study similes (example: as pretty as a picture), metaphors (example: the wind was a bully), and idioms (example: time to hit the sack). • **Practice pages: 59–61**

Your child will find antonyms (example: exhausted/energetic) and synonyms (example: exhausted/drained). • **Practice page: 62**

Your child will learn new words from reading, including specialized words from math, science, history, and other subject areas. • **Practice page: 63**

© Carson-Dellosa • CD-704504

Making Inferences

Read the story. Then, circle the phrase that completes each sentence.

Before the Atkins family began to pack for their vacation, they made a list of what they would need. Then, they laid out the needed clothes on the dining room table. They each had three pairs of shorts, three T-shirts, a swimming suit, socks, and shoes. They put their tents, sleeping bags, raincoats, flashlights, bug spray, cooking equipment, and fishing gear on the dining room floor.

1. The Atkins family's vacation was going ____ .

   to be in a warm climate

   to be in a city

2. On their vacation, they were _____ .

   going to eat out in restaurants

   going camping

3. The place they were going _____ .

   often had afternoon showers

   never had any bugs

4. They would be away _____ .

   for two weeks

   for a long weekend

They put the camping equipment and a duffel bag filled with their clothes in the car. They were off! In a couple of hours, they got to the campsite. After setting up camp, they headed for a swim. They ran shoeless to the water and jumped in. After swimming, they had to shower because they were muddy. They hung their suits on trees to dry. While Mom prepared dinner at the campsite, Dad and the children went back to the lake with their poles and bait.

5. The campsite was _____ .

   at the seashore

   in the woods

6. They swam _____ .

   in a swimming pool

   in a lake

7. The campsite was _____ .

   not too far from home

   first class

8. Dad and the children _____ .

   brought back fish

   fell in the pond

Ask your child to read any paragraph aloud from a favorite chapter book. What questions about characters, settings, and events does the text answer directly? What is suggested or hinted at, but not directly stated?

Themes

Write the letter for the lesson that best describes the theme of each story.

A. If you are patient, your turn will come.

B. If you want to do well, keep practicing.

C. Being brave will help you achieve your goals.

_____ 1. Bethany's friends talked on the phone and traded glittery stickers. Each afternoon, they took turns deciding how to spend their time. Bethany did not always like the activity, but she played anyway. She knew that her turn would arrive soon.

_____ 2. Alex wanted to learn his multiplication tables. His friends knew how to multiply, and he wished that he could do it, too. Each day, he spent one hour studying his flash cards. By the end of the month, Alex was a multiplication expert!

_____ 3. During the school play, Trey was scared to go on stage. But he took a deep breath and stepped onto the stage. He was a star!

Write a short story for each theme.

4. Telling the truth is very important. _____

_____

_____

5. Everyone makes mistakes. _____

_____

_____

6. Even if you lose, you might learn a valuable lesson. _____

_____

_____

Helping at Home

Choose a common theme such as "don't give up" or "good wins over evil." Have fun with your child brainstorming stories that illustrate the theme. Stories may include those found in books, movies, and TV shows. Keep going with another theme.

Characters, Settings, and Events

Read the story below.

The Crow Who Brought the Daylight (An Inuit Story)

Long ago when the earth was first born, the Inuit people from the north lived in darkness. They did not mind because they thought everyone lived in darkness. But one day an old crow let something slip. He had flown all around the world and had seen daylight many times on his travels. When the Inuit people heard about daylight, they wanted it too.

"Think about all of the things we could do if we had daylight," the people said. "We could travel far. We would be safer. We could see polar bears coming. We could catch more fish." The people asked the old crow to fly out and bring them back daylight. He said that he was too old and too tired. But the people continued to beg. Finally, Crow agreed.

Crow flew east for a long time. He had nearly given up when he saw a faint flicker of daylight ahead of him. "Ah," said the tired crow. "There's the daylight the people want." As he continued flying, the sky got brighter and brighter. He finally landed in a tree near a river. He needed to rest after his long journey.

Crow watched a village girl take water from the river. Hoping to get warm, he turned himself into a speck of dust and floated down onto her warm fur coat. When she returned to her father's snow home, Crow floated off the girl's coat and into her young brother's ear. The boy started to cry.

"What's wrong?" his father asked.

"Ask for a ball of daylight to play with," the speck of dust whispered.

The father was glad to give his favorite son a ball of daylight. He wanted him to be happy, and he had plenty of balls of daylight. The boy took the ball of daylight and left his snow home to play outside. That quickly, the speck of dust turned back into Crow again. He grabbed the ball of daylight in his claws and flew quickly up into the bright sky, heading west back to his people.

When he reached the land of the Inuit again, the people were waiting for him. "Quick!" they exclaimed. "Give us daylight!"

"I could only bring one ball back," Crow said. "There is only enough for half the year." The people didn't mind. They were glad for any daylight at all.

Crow dropped the ball to the ground, where it splintered into a thousand pieces of daylight. As the pieces shone upward, the land of the Inuit became bright and beautiful. The people could see for miles and miles. What a beautiful homeland they had!

4/24/15

Characters, Settings, and Events

Answer the questions with complete sentences.

1. On the previous page, draw an illustration for the story. Write a caption beneath it.

2. What are three things you could not do if you lived in total darkness?

_____

_____

3. Why do you think Crow was willing to go on such a long journey?

_____

_____

4. What would be the advantage to being able to change your shape like Crow did when he changed himself into a speck of dust? Explain.

_____ cornfat _____ climed

_____ vines ally

good

5. Do you think a ball of daylight would be heavy or light? Explain.

_____

_____

6. Where do the Inuit people live? Use reference materials if you need to.

_____

_____

_____

Helping at Home

Ask your child to draw a detailed illustration of a favorite scene from a book or movie. Admire the finished artwork and ask, "What details about the story's characters, settings, and events are reflected in your illustration?"

Compare and Contrast

Read the summary of *Shiloh* by Phyllis Reynolds Naylor (Aladdin, 2000). Use details from the summary to complete the puzzle. The bold spaces will tell you what award this book received.

In *Shiloh*, an award-winning book, 11-year-old Marty Preston tells about what happens when a dog follows him home. Marty lives with his parents and two sisters, Becky and Dara Lynn, in the hills above Friendly. Friendly is a small town in West Virginia near Sisterville. On a Sunday afternoon, after a big dinner of rabbit and sweet potatoes, Marty goes for a walk along the river. During his walk, Marty spies a short-haired dog. The dog, a beagle with black and brown spots, does not make a sound as he watches and follows Marty. From the dog's behavior, Marty suspects that the dog has been mistreated. Since he found the dog near the old Shiloh schoolhouse, Marty calls the dog Shiloh. Marty soon discovers that Shiloh belongs to mean Judd Travers. After returning Shiloh to Judd, Marty contemplates how he can earn enough money to buy the dog. Before Marty can solve this problem, he is faced with a difficult decision.

1. In what town does Marty live?

2. How old is Marty?

3. What kind of potatoes does the family eat on Sunday?

4. What kind of meat do they eat?

5. What kind of dog is Shiloh?

6. Write the last name of Shiloh's owner.

7. Name one of Marty's sisters.

8. What adjective is used to describe Judd Travers?

9. What is Marty's last name?

10. On what day does Marty find Shiloh?

11. Who tells the story?

12. Marty finds the dog by what schoolhouse?

Compare and Contrast

This book summary is about the much beloved book *Old Yeller* by Fred Gipson (Scholastic Book Services, 1957). *Old Yeller* won a number of awards, including the 1957 Newbery Honor Book award.

Old Yeller is about a boy and a dog. When Travis's father left to take their cattle to market, young Travis had to take his father's place on the farm. This required him to plow the fields, chop wood, hunt for food for the dinner table, take care of the livestock, and protect his mother and little brother. This was a lot of responsibility for young Travis and sometimes he did not feel up to it. In the middle of all this, an ugly yellow dog showed up on the farm. At first, Travis hated the dog for stealing the family's meager supply of meat. But later, after the dog saved his little brother from an angry mother bear, Travis came to appreciate the dog's protection and help. He named the dog Old Yeller and the dog became his closest friend. At the end of the story, Old Yeller was bitten by a rabid wolf and Travis had a hard decision to make.

Compare and contrast what you read about *Old Yeller* with the summary of *Shiloh* on the previous page.

1. What are some qualities that Shiloh and Old Yeller have in common?

_____

_____

2. Compare and contrast how the two boys met the dogs that were to become their best friends.

_____

_____

3. Tell what you know or might guess about the difficult decisions both Marty and Travis had to make at the end of these books.

_____

_____

_____

Helping at Home

Ask your child to think of another familiar story about a young person and his or her special animal friend. It could be from a book or a movie. Listen as your child compares and contrasts that story with the summaries of *Shiloh* and *Old Yeller.*

Characters, Settings, and Events

Read the story and follow the directions.

There was an old lady who lived on the edge of town. Everyone referred to her as Granny. Because she kept to herself, she seemed a little different to some. She asked nothing of anyone and did nothing for anyone except her many dogs. The number of dogs varied daily. Some dogs came only when they were hungry and left until they returned to eat again. Some knew that it was a good home and stayed.

One day, the paper boy noticed that Granny's papers had not been picked up for three or four days. The dogs in her yard were thin and looked almost lifeless as they moved about slowly. He had not seen Granny for about a week. He wondered if she was all right.

He got off his bike and walked up the steps onto the front porch. He walked around and peered in the windows, but he did not see anything. he opened the front door slightly and called, "Hello! Anyone here?" He listened for a minute. He thought that he heard a whimpering sound, so he quickly rode to the closest neighbor's house and called 911.

When the police arrived, they found that Granny had fallen and had not been able to move to call for help. The paramedics determined that Granny needed to go to the hospital, where she stayed for a few days.

While she was in the hospital, the paper boy came to feed her dogs every day. When Granny came home, neighbors brought food and flowers. Granny was sorry that she had not gotten to know her new friends sooner, but she was glad that she had now "found" them.

1. Circle what Granny's behavior indicates about her character at the beginning of the story.

   She prefers to be alone.   She does not like people.   She is mean.

2. How does Granny's behavior change?

   _____

3. Write three adjectives that describe the paper boy's character.

   _____   _____   _____

Ask your child to describe a character, setting, or event from a favorite book. Praise your child's good memory of the story, then have him or her look in the actual book for specific words, sentences, and passages that confirm the description.

Context Clues

Use context clues to complete each sentence with one of the words in parentheses.

1. _____ is one of Tom's favorite subjects. (Astronaut, Astronomy, Atmosphere)

2. He _____ liked to follow the movement of the stars. (especially, establish, exceptionally)

3. When Tom was a little boy, his favorite outing was to visit a nearby _____. (platform, planetarium, planet)

4. Tom was delighted when his family gave him a _____. (telegram, telephoned, telescope)

5. Part of his birthday present was to go camping with his father in a park where _____ were good for stargazing. (constellations, conditions, conjunctions)

6. When the night came for Tom to go to the park, he took the necessary equipment with which to make his _____. (observes, orbits, observations)

7. Tom saw several _____, including Orion and the Dippers. (consultants, constellations, conformations)

8. Tom also saw the North Star, which is almost exactly _____ the north pole. (over, other, off)

9. He drew pictures of what he saw and recorded their positions using a _____. (compass, confess, congress)

10. He had a wonderful time and asked if his father would take him on another _____ to observe the stars. (explore, expedition, experience)

Helping at Home

For several items from this page, ask your child to explain the thinking process he or she used to choose one of the words to fill in the blank. Ask your child to underline words in the sentence that provided a context clue.

Reading Poetry

Read the poems aloud to another person.

'Tis Midnight

1 'Tis midnight, and the setting sun
  Is slowly rising in the west;
The rapid rivers slowly run,
  The frog is on his downy nest.
The pensive goat and sportive cow
  Hilarious, leap from bough to bough.

Anonymous

The Train Pulled in the Station

2 O, the train pulled in the station,
  The bell was ringing wet;
The track ran by the depot,
  And I think it's running yet.

3 'Twas midnight on the ocean,
  Not a streetcar was in sight;
The sun and moon were shining,
  And it rained all day that night.

4 'Twas a summer day in winter,
  And the snow was raining fast;
As a barefoot boy, with shoes on,
  Stood, sitting on the grass.

5 O, I jumped into the river,
  Just because it had a bed;
I took a sheet of water
  For to cover up my head.

6 O, the rain makes all things beautiful,
  The flowers and grasses too;
If the rain makes all things beautiful,
  Why don't it rain on you?

An American Folk Song

Reading Poetry

Refer back to the poem on page 18, "The Train Pulled in the Station." For each stanza, write one thing that doesn't make sense.

1. Stanza 1 _____

2. Stanza 2 _____

3. Stanza 3 _____

4. Stanza 4 _____

5. Stanza 5 _____

Write what you think is the silliest part of "'Tis Midnight." Be sure to tell why you think it's silly.

6. _____

_____

Write the words that make up the compound words found in the stanzas in parentheses.

7. (3) _____ and _____ ,

_____ and _____

8. (4) _____ and _____

Check the meaning of the underlined homograph as it is used in the sentence.

9. <u>Dates</u> are often used when making muffins.

_____ a kind of fruit   _____ a day in a month

10. The holy man went on a <u>fast</u>.

_____ swift moving   _____ a period of not eating food

11. Cheese can <u>age</u> rapidly.

_____ to grow old   _____ long period of time

12. It was almost more than his mother could <u>bear</u>.

_____ put up with   _____ a large omnivorous animal

Helping at Home

Think of a topic that interests your child such as horses, shipwrecks, or football. What details about the topic might be included in a poem? What might be explored in a dramatic play? What about the topic would make a good focus for a prose article or essay?

Point of View

Read the following passages and choose the point of view of each (first person, third person). Then, list the characters in the story, using the word *author* for stories written in the first person.

My family flies out tomorrow morning for a week's vacation at Yellowstone National Park. How exciting! But I have a problem. I am somewhat afraid of the wild animals that are allowed to roam free in the park. I know this is good for them, but the idea of meeting a buffalo or a bear or a gray wolf on one of the trails scares me to death. Please don't mention this to anyone.

1. Point of view _____

2. Characters in the story _____

Tony and Jose decided to order a different kind of pizza. Usually, they preferred sausage or pepperoni toppings. No veggies! No strange ingredients! They agreed to order every third ingredient from the list of possible choices until they had five items. When the list was complete, Tony looked at Jose and said, "You get the side with the anchovies and duck!" Jose wrinkled his nose and said, "Well, then you get the side with the red beets and green peas!"

3. Point of view _____

4. Characters in the story _____

When Erin made a list of kids to invite to her party, she thought about a couple of things. First, how many kids did she want for her party? If it is to be a sleep-over, she might only want four or five. If it is to be an outing at a frozen yogurt store, she might be allowed to invite a lot more. Then, she thought about who her best friends are. Whose feelings would be hurt if they aren't invited? Who might not want to come? And, who always invites her to their parties? There were lots of decisions to make.

5. Point of view _____

6. Characters in the story _____

Helping at Home

When your child shares a story about something that happened to him or her, observe that it was told in first person. Challenge your child to tell the same story again in third person and yet again in first person from the point of view of another person involved.

Main Idea

Read the following passage and complete the activity below.

Ancient civilizations did not have scientific information that explained the causes of earthquakes. They made up stories that reveal their lack of understanding. One belief of some of these ancient people was that Earth was carried on the backs of animals.

Some Native Americans thought that a giant sea turtle held up Earth. They believed that when the turtle moved, Earth moved. When the turtle moved more, Earth moved more, causing cracks to form on Earth's surface.

In India, it was believed that four elephants held up Earth. They stood on the back of a turtle, and the turtle, in turn, balanced on the back of a snake. If any of these animals moved, Earth would shake and cause an earthquake. The greater the movement was, the greater the earthquake was.

The ancient Greeks thought that earthquakes showed the gods' anger. A giant, named Atlas, had rebelled against the gods, so he had to hold the world on his shoulders as punishment. The Greeks believed that any time Atlas adjusted Earth's weight on his shoulders, an earthquake followed.

Write the main idea of the passage. Then, write a supporting idea from each of the last three paragraphs.

1. _____

    _____

2. _____

    _____

3. _____

    _____

4. _____

    _____

Helping at Home

Encourage your child to write another paragraph for the article on this page. It should support the main idea and add new supporting details. The new paragraph might explain a modern understanding of earthquakes.

Main Idea and Details

Read the passage.

Taking Care of Teeth

Long ago, people cleaned their teeth in many interesting ways. They scratched their teeth with sticks, wiped them with rags, or even chewed on crushed bones or shells. Tooth care has come a long way in the past few hundred years. Now we have fluoride toothpaste, dental floss, and specially angled toothbrushes to keep our teeth healthy.

It took someone with a lot of time on his hands to invent the first toothbrush. In the 1770s, a man named William Addis was in prison. While he was wiping his teeth with a rag, he had the idea to make a tool for cleaning teeth. He used a bone and some bristles from a hairbrush. He carefully drilled holes in one end of the bone. Then, he trimmed the brush bristles and pushed them into the holes that he had drilled. He glued the bristles into place and had made the first toothbrush.

People have used different tooth cleaners over the years. Many cleaners, such as crushed bones and shells, actually damaged the protective enamel on teeth. Chalk was a popular cleaner in the 1850s. Baking soda was also used for many years because it was abrasive. Some toothpastes still contain baking soda. Other people used salt as a tooth cleaner. Many of today's toothpastes contain sodium, too. Fluoride was first added to toothpaste in 1956. Fluoride greatly reduced the number of cavities in children. More recently, calcium was added to toothpaste in the 1960s to help strengthen teeth.

Using dental floss once a day is one of the most important things that you can do for your teeth. Originally, the thin string was made of silk. Now, dental floss comes in different colors and flavors, tape, and waxed and unwaxed varieties. Dental floss removes "interproximal plaque accumulation," which means that it scrapes off the plaque between your teeth where a toothbrush cannot reach.

The inventions and improvements in dental care have helped people maintain stronger, healthier teeth. We now know how to care for our teeth every day.

Main Idea and Details

Use the passage on page 22 to answer the questions.

1. Why did the author write this passage?

    A. to entertain

    B. to teach

    C. to sell something

2. What kind of passage is "Taking Care of Teeth"?

    A. a factual passage

    B. a humorous passage

    C. a fictional passage

3. Why was calcium added to toothpaste? _____

   _____

4. What does fluoride do? _____

   _____

5. Complete the diagram with details from the passage.

The Importance of Dental Floss	William Addis
A. _____ _____	A. _____ B. _____

Tooth Care

Tooth Cleaners Over the Years	Tooth Cleaning Today
A. _____ B. _____ C. _____	A. _____ B. _____ C. _____

Helping at Home Encourage your child to read a newspaper, magazine, or online article about a topic that he or she finds interesting. Ask your child to share three details from the article. Then ask, "What main idea do those details support?"

Visual Aids in Text

Read the poem. Then, read the passage.

Days of the Week

Monday's Child

Monday's child is fair of face,
Tuesday's child is full of **grace**,
Wednesday's child will fear no foe,
Thursday's child has far to go,
Friday's child is loving and giving,
Saturday's child works hard for a living,
But a child that's born on the Sabbath day
Is **bonny** and **blithe** and good in every way.

Anonymous

No one seems to agree on the **origin** of the seven-day week. Many historians believe that the Babylonians were the first to break the year into months. At some point in history, it became important to divide the year into smaller parts. Around 1600 BC, a new period of time was created. It was longer than a day, but less than a month. This was called the week.

A lunar month is the time that it takes the moon to complete a cycle from new moon to new moon. A lunar month is $29\frac{1}{2}$ days. One reason a week is seven days long is because four seven-day weeks are close to the amount of time in a lunar month.

Different **cultures** have had different names for the days of the week. However, names of the month are similar in many languages.

In ancient times, people could see seven "planets" in the sky without a telescope. They saw the sun, the moon, Mars, Mercury, Jupiter, Venus, and Saturn. (No one had studied the sky with a telescope until Galileo in the sixteenth century. Until then, people thought that the sun and the moon were planets.)

Many languages connect each day of the week with one of these planets. In English, you can find these planet names in Monday, Saturday, and Sunday. The other four days have been substituted with the names of Nordic and Anglo-Saxon gods.

English	French	Planet
Monday	lundi	moon
Tuesday	mardi	Mars
Wednesday	mercredi	Mercury
Thursday	jeudi	Jupiter
Friday	vendredi	Venus
Saturday	samedi	Saturn
Sunday	dimanche	sun

Visual Aids in Text

Use the poem and the passage on page 24 to answer the questions.

1. Write the sentence from the passage that tells when people began to use instruments to look at the sky. _____

   _____

2. What is the French word for Thursday? _____

3. What are the names of the "planets" that could be seen without a telescope?

   _____

4. What planet was Saturday named after? _____

5. Describe the child born on Friday. _____

Write the letter of the definition on the line next to its matching word. Use a dictionary for help.

6. _____ bonny   A. merry

7. _____ grace   B. beginning

8. _____ blithe   C. attractive

9. _____ cultures   D. civilizations

10. _____ origin   E. having charm

Complete the outline with details from the passage.

11. Months and weeks

    A. Babylonians separate years into months.

    B. _____

12. Names of days

    A. Ancient people named days after planets.

    B. _____

Helping at Home
Encourage your child to use the text on page 24 as well as additional research to add a fourth column to the chart at the bottom of the page. The new column should list the names of ancient gods that some days of the week are named after.

Making a Chart

Read the information. Then, complete the chart.

Mollusks belong to a large family of invertebrate animals. Animals that belong to this group usually have soft, one-sectioned bodies that are covered by hard shells. A person walking on a beach might find several of their discarded shells. Animals once lived in these seashells.

Biologists divide mollusks into seven groups called classes, but only some of the mollusks have hard protective shells. Gastropoda is one class of mollusks. Most often, a gastropod has a single, coiled shell. Included in this class are limpets, slugs, snails, and whelks. They can be found on the beaches of the Atlantic and Pacific Oceans in North America.

Bivalves is another large class of mollusks. The shell of a bivalve is actually two shells hinged together at one end or along one side. The animals that call these shells home include clams, oysters, mussels, and scallops. They too can be found on both coasts of North America.

A third class of mollusks are chitons. A chiton's body is covered by eight shell plates that look something like a turtle's shell. Merten's chiton, northern red chiton, and mossy mopalia are all included in this class. Chitons generally live in shallow rock pools. They can be found along the shores of the Pacific Ocean from Alaska to Mexico.

	Gastropods	**Bivalves**	**Chitons**
What do their shells look like?			
Where can they be found?			
List mollusks included in each class.			

Helping at Home

Look through a print or online newspaper with your child. Notice what information is given in paragraphs and what facts are presented in charts, graphs, maps, or other formats. Talk about how to read graphics and why they are useful.

Words in Text

Read the passage. Then, write each bold word next to its definition below.

Food for Survival

The rocky land of the northern forests in North America was never good for farming. Without fish and game, the early **natives** would have starved. Their lives were **contingent** on the animals they hunted.

In order to survive, the early Native Americans of the North American forests played games that **incorporated** the skills they needed to be successful in their **culture**. They needed to be able to judge distances, pick up clues and signs from their environment, and conceal themselves from the animals they hunted. In one of the games the Native Americans played, the men threw axes. In another, they took turns throwing spears or sticks into a hoop on the ground. Such games improved the players' **accuracy**.

Moose and caribou were very important to the tribes. Moose usually lived and traveled by themselves. Caribou migrated in herds covering a large territory each season. The Native Americans **stalked** the moose from one **range** to another, but when hunting caribou, they would wait for them at a place along the caribou's trails.

Weirs, nets, traps, hooks, and spears were used to catch fish. Whitefish and jackfish were caught in lakes, and Arctic grayling and trout were caught in rivers. The Native Americans fished from the shore or in canoes in summer and through holes cut in the ice in winter.

After the ice melted, the traps were set. Sometimes, the Native Americans would discover a bear still hibernating in its den. Such a kill would feed the camp for a few days. Sometimes, when meat was scarce, the Native Americans would eat rabbit, mink, or wolverine. When hunting became poor, they lived on dried meat and fish and on pemmican, a mixture of dried meat and animal fat.

1. open area on which animals roam _____

2. combined into one body _____

3. original inhabitants _____

4. dependent upon _____

5. pursued prey _____

6. quality of being exact _____

7. enclosures set in a waterway for catching fish _____

8. one's social group _____

© Carson-Dellosa • CD-704504

Helping at Home

Encourage your child to seek out and read a nonfiction book about a topic of interest. After reading, ask your child to make a short glossary that defines 10 key words from the book. Slip the glossary in the back of the book for other readers to use.

Reading a Chart

Use the chart to answer the questions.

	Area (in sq. mi.)	Highest Mountain (in feet)	Lowest Point (feet below sea level)	Longest River (in miles)
Africa	11,700,000	Kilimanjaro (19,340)	Lake Assal (512)	Nile (4,145)
Antarctica	5,400,000	Vinson Massif (16,864)	not known	no rivers
Asia	17,200,000	Mount Everest (29,028)	Dead Sea (1,312)	Yangtze (3,915)
Australia	3,071,000	Mount Kosciusko (7,310)	Lake Eyre (52)	Murray-Darling (2,310)
Europe	3,580,000	Elbrus (18,510)	Caspian Sea (92)	Volga (2,194)
North America	9,400,000	Mount McKinley (20,320)	Death Valley (282)	Missouri (2,540)
South America	6,900,000	Aconcagua (22,834)	Valdes Peninsula (131)	Amazon (4,000)

1. Which continent has the highest mountain and the lowest point?

_____

2. What are the two longest rivers? _____

3. Which continents are about the same size? _____

4. Which continent has the shortest mountain and the highest lowest point?

_____

5. List the mountains that are greater than 20,000 feet high.

_____

Helping at Home

Encourage your child to research the name of the largest city on each continent and its population. The information can be used to create a fifth column for the chart on this page. Have your child write a question for you to answer based on the new information.

Reading a Time Line

Dinosaurs lived long ago—about 60 million years ago. Today, all that is left of them are their fossils, bones, and footprints. But, what does 60 million years mean to us? A geologic time scale was developed by scientists that illustrates the periods in Earth's history. It can help those of us living today gain some perspective about the time involved in the development of life on Earth.

Read the chart and answer the questions.

1. Earth's history is divided into how many major eras? _____

2. What are the era's names?

_____

3. In which era did the dinosaurs exist?

_____

_____

4. Into how many periods is the Mesozoic era divided?

_____

5. What are the Mesozoic periods' names?

_____

6. In which era do you live?

_____

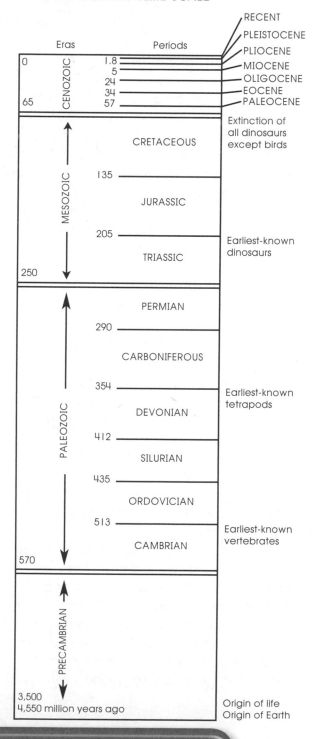

GEOLOGIC AND EVOLUTIONARY TIME SCALE

Eras	Periods	
CENOZOIC	0 / 1.8 / 5 / 24 / 34 / 57 / 65	RECENT, PLEISTOCENE, PLIOCENE, MIOCENE, OLIGOCENE, EOCENE, PALEOCENE
MESOZOIC	CRETACEOUS / 135 / JURASSIC / 205 / TRIASSIC / 250	Extinction of all dinosaurs except birds / Earliest-known dinosaurs
PALEOZOIC	PERMIAN / 290 / CARBONIFEROUS / 354 / DEVONIAN / 412 / SILURIAN / 435 / ORDOVICIAN / 513 / CAMBRIAN / 570	Earliest-known tetrapods / Earliest-known vertebrates
PRECAMBRIAN	3,500 / 4,550 million years ago	Origin of life / Origin of Earth

Helping at Home

Talk about ways to organize information. Brainstorm facts that could be organized by time order (example: a weekly menu), by cause/effect (example: science experiments), by problem/solution (example: a story from history), etc.

Reading in Content Areas

Read the passage.

The Scent of Night

Gourmet meals for moths and bats

1   A scent…an aroma…a smell—this is all a moth needs to find one of the many flowers that bloom as the sun sets. Unlike colorful butterflies or honeybees, the drab hawk moth and the little brown bat seek nectar at night.

2   Plants that flower by day need diurnal animals to help with pollination. Plants that bloom at night rely on nocturnal animals for the same reason. Pollen is a powdery substance inside flowers. Pollination occurs when pollen is moved from a flower on one plant to a flower on another plant. Without pollination, plants cannot make seeds for the next year. Most brightly colored flowers close their petals at night to keep their pollen dry. In the morning, after the night's dew has evaporated, the petals reopen. They are ready again for visits from tiny insects and birds.

   Take a visit to a garden at sunset. If you are lucky, you might see a daytime bug that has been trapped in a flower as its petals closed. Don't worry. The bug will be snug until the next morning.

3   Night-blooming flowers come in shades of pale white, yellow, and pink. They lack the dazzling colors of day bloomers because animals are not attracted to them by sight. Animals find these flowers by smell. Their fragrance during the day is often faint or unnoticeable. At night, however, a single blossom can fill an entire garden with its scent.

Honeysuckle

4   This vine has trumpet-shaped flowers and grows wild all over the world. Its creamy white and yellow blossoms make a gourmet meal for the hawk moth. Like the butterfly, this moth has a long proboscis that is perfect for sipping the flower's honey-flavored nectar.

5   If you have a honeysuckle plant near your house, visit it on a warm, moonlit night. Carefully remove a blossom by pinching off the slender stem at the bottom of the flower. With your fingernail, nip the green base of the flower in half. Gently pull back on the base until you see a drop of liquid. This is the flower's nectar.

Wild Banana Flower

6   Most night-flowering plants are pleasant for humans to smell. But there are some you just don't want to get near. The purple/brownish flower of the wild banana has rust-colored pollen. By its second day of blooming, it has a scent that reminds people of rotting meat. Silky brown bats are so attracted to this smell that they sometimes get trapped inside the flower's huge, stinky petals when they close at sunrise. What a way to spend the day!

Reading in Content Areas

1. The wild banana flower stinks. What is the

   effect? _____

   _____

2. Do nocturnal or diurnal animals

   pollinate night-blooming plants? _____

   _____

3. Why are night-blooming plants so pale?

   _____

   _____

4. What helps the hawk moth get nectar out

   of the honeysuckle flower? _____

   _____

5. Why do you think day-blooming plants
   need to keep their pollen dry? (Hint: Think
   of how the powdery pollen is transported.)

   _____

   _____

6. The author has two opinions in paragraph 6.

   Write one of them. _____

   _____

Write the letter of the definition in front of each word. Use a dictionary if you need help.

7. _____ drab   A. special, tasty

8. _____ dew   B. to look for something

9. _____ stinky   C. a reddish-brown color

10. _____ evaporate D. drops of water

11. _____ fragrance E. to clip or snip

12. _____ seek   F. to dry up

13. _____ rely   G. to be smelly

14. _____ gourmet   H. scent; aroma

15. _____ nip   I. colorless

16. _____ rust   J. to depend on

17. If the suffix *re-* means "do again," what
    does *reopen* mean?

    _____

18. If the suffix *un-* means "not," what does
    the word *unnoticeable* mean?

    _____

Encourage your child to wonder about how something works. It could be a cell phone, the human eye, or a political process. Ask your child to read and research to answer his or her questions and write a short explanation, including visual aids.

Firsthand and Secondhand Accounts

Read the story. Then, follow the directions on the following page.

Gerbils can be wonderful pets. But, like any pet, they require commitment. New owners must consider if they have the time and the motivation to give good care. It is important to consider timing, money, and circumstances.

Gerbils weigh from 60 to 100 grams, about the same as half a medium baked potato. They grow to be about four inches long. Their tails are around the same length. They come in different colors, but most of them have white fur on their stomachs. They can live up to four years.

The basics for setting up a gerbil as a pet at home include a cage, gerbil food, toys and treats, and litter and bedding materials. It will cost money to raise a healthy and happy gerbil. A cage can cost $25 or more. A year's worth of gerbil food, toys, litter, and bedding can cost $300 or more. Veterinarian bills can add up. Save your allowance!

Gerbils are busy little creatures. They can be very active and love to play. Gerbil toys such as exercise wheels, play tubes, ladders, and run-around balls offer these playful pets hours of fun. Gerbils love to dig. They can get hours of tunneling fun in extra bedding, shredded paper towels, or hay.

It is helpful to remember that gerbils are social creatures. Buying them two at a time can add to the happy gerbil home. They should be introduced to each other while young to make certain they get along. Ideally, the two will come from the same family. Remember not to pair a female and male to avoid litters of new gerbils.

Gerbil food is usually made up of grain, seeds, pellets, and dried vegetables. Gerbils especially find sunflower seeds tasty treats, so they may pick these out and eat them first! It is also recommended that gerbils receive small bits of chopped vegetables such as lettuce, carrots, and broccoli. Because a rodent's teeth grow continuously, it needs something to gnaw on to wear them down. A sterile bone or safe twig should be included in its daily fare. And, like all pets, gerbils need a good supply of fresh water, changed daily.

A pet gerbil can offer hours of fun and lots of cuddles. They are small creatures and must be handled carefully, but with daily care and attention, they are soon a valued part of the family.

Firsthand and Secondhand Accounts

After reading the passage on page 32, interview someone who owns or has owned a gerbil. Ask these questions:

1. When did you get a gerbil? _____

2. Did you like having a gerbil for a pet? _____

3. Was it a lot of work or was it easy to take care of a gerbil? _____

4. What did your gerbil eat? _____

5. Did your gerbil like to play? With what? _____

6. Did it cost much to take care of a pet gerbil? _____

7. What didn't you like about owning a gerbil? _____

8. Would you recommend a gerbil for a pet? _____

Now, write a paragraph to compare and contrast the passage on page 32 with the facts you learned in your interview. Which gave you the best information?

_____

_____

_____

_____

_____

_____

_____

_____

_____

_____

Helping at Home Ask your child to gather firsthand and secondhand accounts about being in fourth grade. He or she might interview older people about fourth grade memories or read *Fourth Grade Rats* by Jerry Spinelli. Ask your child to compare the accounts.

Cause and Effect

Write the letter of the effect for each cause.

1. After the tsunami hit Japan, _____

2. When kids are bullied, _____

3. If you don't floss your teeth, _____

4. Fewer people buy from stores _____

5. While traveling in large cities with the windows down, _____

6. When you sit in the back seat of the bus, _____

7. The airport was closed _____

8. A solar eclipse happens when _____

9. Hundreds of people were stranded _____

10. Many people go to the emergency room _____

11. After Harriet Tubman fled slavery, _____

12. Yeast produces gas in bread, _____

13. Helen Keller had a childhood illness _____

14. Peer pressure _____

15. Good test grades are easier to get _____

A. due to heavy rain and poor visibility.

B. when doctor's offices are closed.

C. they become depressed and unhappy.

D. if you study before tests.

E. can make students uncomfortable.

F. the ride will be bumpier.

G. because of heavy snowfall.

H. that left her deaf and blind.

I. she helped rescue other slaves.

J. many people donated food and clothing.

K. causing it to rise.

L. since it became easy to shop online.

M. you might get cavities.

N. the moon moves between Earth and the sun.

O. you can often smell air pollution.

Helping at Home Ask your child to combine and write several items from this page as complete statements of cause and effect. The statements should include some of the following words: *if…then, because, when…then, why, so, since, as a result.*

Compare and Contrast

Read the passage. Then, write a paragraph comparing and contrasting the two players.

Michael Jordan grew up in North Carolina. His father built a basketball court in the backyard for all of his children to use. Michael enjoyed all sports, but basketball was his favorite. Michael tried to make his high school's varsity team as a sophomore, but the coach thought that he was too short. However, by his junior year, he had grown and sharpened his basketball skills, and he make the varsity team. The rest is history: he got a scholarship to the University of North Carolina, won the national championship for the university, helped the United States Olympic basketball team win a gold medal, and became a Chicago Bull. Michael Jordan broke many National Basketball Association (NBA) records and received several Most Valuable Player (MVP) awards. He retired from basketball and tried playing baseball, but after two years, he returned to playing basketball and set even more records.

Kareem Abdul-Jabbar was born Ferdinand Lewis "Lew" Alcindor, Jr. He was born and raised in the New York City area. Early on, he had a passion for music and baseball. Not until the summer between first and second grade did he first pick up a basketball. In eighth grade, he helped his junior high win the district championship. Lew made the high school varsity team his freshman year, and the rest is history: he led his high school to record-setting winning streaks, received a scholarship to the University of California at Los Angeles, and led the team to three titles while receiving three MVP awards. During his college years, he changed his name to Kareem Abdul-Jabbar. He also boycotted the 1968 Olympics. He and other US athletes decided a boycott would send a message about racism in the United States. After college, he was drafted by the Milwaukee Bucks and was traded six years later to the Los Angeles Lakers. For both teams, he had personal and team successes. He was voted MVP five times. He was the NBA's leading scorer and led both teams to national championships.

_____

_____

_____

_____

_____

_____

Helping at Home

Have your child choose two pets, friends, games, or other subjects to compare in a Venn diagram. Brainstorm characteristics of each to write in the circles and shared characteristics to write in the overlapping part of the drawing.

Writing an Opinion

Imagine that your teacher has decided to rearrange students' desks. Should students be allowed to choose where they sit in class? Use the graphic organizer to help you plan your persuasive paragraph.

What is your opinion on the topic?

_____

_____

_____

Whom are you trying to persuade?

_____

_____

_____

Why do you think that others should agree with your opinion? List three reasons to support your opinion.

1. _____

   _____

2. _____

   _____

3. _____

   _____

Use your notes to help you write a five-sentence persuasive paragraph. Include a closing statement that restates your opinion.

_____

_____

_____

_____

Helping at Home

Talk about what it means to "play devil's advocate." Challenge your child to think of three reasons that could be used to support the opposite opinion about the issue stated on this page. Why is it important to consider opinions opposite from your own?

Writing an Opinion

Choose a topic. Use the graphic organizer to help you plan a persuasive essay.

What is your opinion on the topic?

_____

_____

_____

Whom are you trying to persuade?

_____

_____

_____

Why do you think that others should agree with your opinion? List three reasons to support your opinion.

1. _____

2. _____

3. _____

To convince the reader, add supporting details for each reason.

1. _____

_____

2. _____

_____

3. _____

_____

On another piece of paper, use your notes to help you write a five-paragraph persuasive essay. Include three reasons, in addition to introductory and concluding paragraphs. Use linking words and phrases such as *for instance, in order to, in addition,* and *as well as.*

Helping at Home

Talk about what makes a good topic for persuasive writing. It should be one that arouses strong opinions and can be viewed from multiple perspectives. Look through a newspaper with your child or watch a documentary and think of possible topics.

37

Examples and Details

Many students love the summer. Think about the summer and why this time of year is special. Complete the chart with examples and details that support the two reasons.

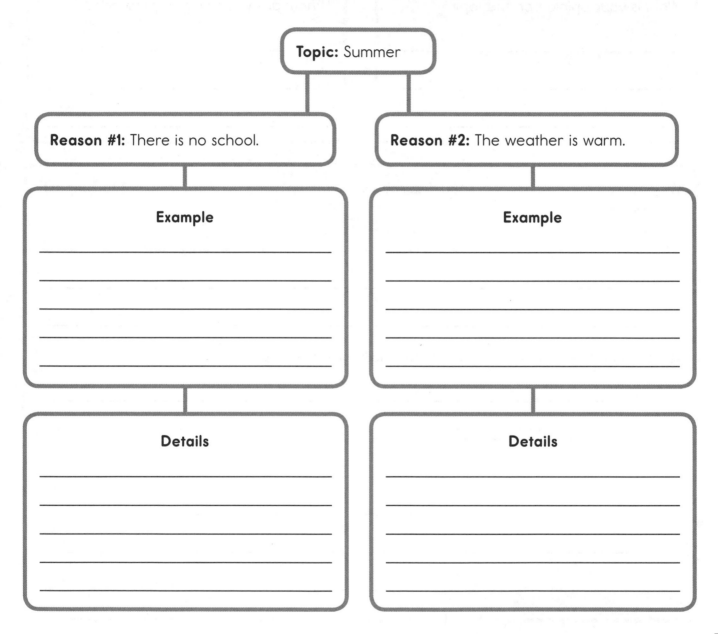

Topic: Summer

Reason #1: There is no school.

Reason #2: The weather is warm.

Example

_____
_____
_____
_____
_____

Example

_____
_____
_____
_____
_____

Details

_____
_____
_____
_____
_____

Details

_____
_____
_____
_____
_____

Helping at Home

Give details and examples about summer and ask your child to tell which reason from this page they could be used to support. You could include facts about temperatures, ideas for summer activities, or stories from summers past.

Writing to Inform

Follow the directions to write an informative essay.

1. Choose a significant current event. Research the topic using the Internet, an encyclopedia, or other books. Make notes about the topic in the table.

Topic: _____

Introduction: _____

_____

Body: _____

_____

_____

_____

Conclusion: _____

_____

2. Include vocabulary that a reader must know to understand your topic. Write at least three important words and their definitions.

_____

_____

_____

3. Use words and phrases to link ideas, such as *above all, actually, also, another, as well as, for example, because, in addition to, in conclusion, last but not least, to begin with.*

4. Use this information to write a first draft of your essay on another sheet of paper.

5. Include an illustration of a main event from your topic.

© Carson-Dellosa • CD-704504

Helping at Home

Ask your child to read his or her first draft to family members as a news report. Encourage listeners to ask questions, make comments, and add information. Ask your child if any comments provided ideas about how to improve the piece.

Revising and Editing

Use this checklist to analyze the first draft of your current events essay from page 39. Note any necessary changes on your first draft. Then, type your final draft on the computer or write it on another sheet of paper. Keep your first and final drafts together.

_____ My essay has a main topic.

_____ My essay is about a significant current event.

_____ I have included essential facts and details.

_____ I have listed details that support the main idea.

_____ I have used vocabulary that fits the topic.

_____ I have given my essay an interesting title.

_____ My essay has an introduction, a body, and a conclusion.

_____ The sentences are complete sentences.

_____ I have used an interesting mix of vocabulary, including active verbs and descriptive adjectives and adverbs.

_____ I have used proper punctuation where needed.

_____ I have checked that all of the words are spelled correctly.

_____ I have capitalized all proper words.

Writing to Inform

Choose a topic. Research it carefully using books, the Internet, and encyclopedias. Fill out the graphic organizer. Then, use the information to write a paragraph about your topic.

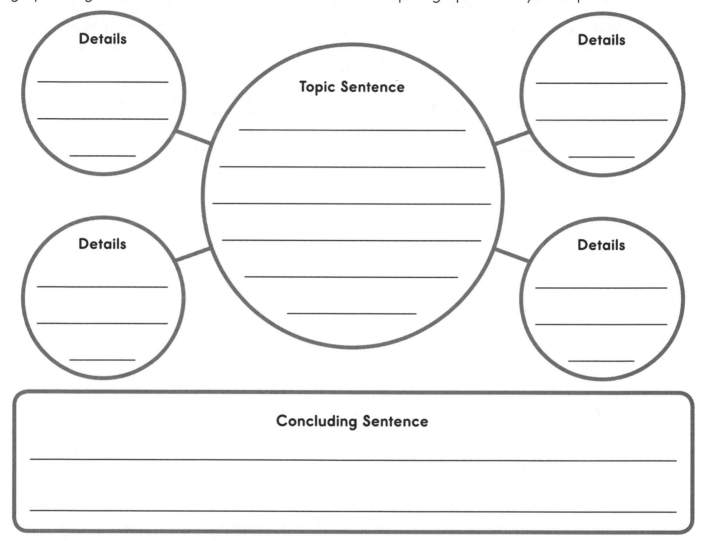

Concluding Sentence

Using this information, write a five-sentence paragraph that tells about the topic.

Choose a paragraph from a feature-length news article or a nonfiction book. Using information from the paragraph, ask your child to make a topic sentence/details organizer like the one at the top of this page.

Writing Directions

Imagine that someone has asked you for the directions to make your favorite sandwich. Help them by writing the steps. Use at least six time-order words. Examples are given in the word bank.

eventually	last	shortly after
finally	next	soon
first	now	then

How to Make My Favorite _____ Sandwich

_____

_____

_____

_____

_____

_____

_____

_____

_____

_____

_____

_____

_____

_____

Helping at Home

Allow five minutes for both you and your child to write a paragraph about how to tie a shoe or do some other simple everyday task. Read each paragraph aloud and have the listener try to follow the directions. Which set of directions was more precise?

Sensory Words

Imagine that you woke up one morning and were 10 feet (3 meters) tall. What would you do if you were that tall? Write a terrific beginning for a story using onomatopoeia (sound words) or the five senses (hearing, sight, touch, taste, and smell). Use words from the word bank to help.

Onomatopoeia Word Bank	Five Senses Word Bank
bang	appeared
honk	looked
screech	saw
crash	felt
giggle	heard
sigh	touched

_____

_____

_____

_____

_____

_____

_____

_____

_____

_____

_____

_____

Helping at Home

Challenge your child to make a new word bank like the one at the top of this page. It should contain words that would be appropriate to use for a story in which the main character wakes up to find that he or she is three inches tall.

Writing Dialogue

Use each dialogue to make an inference. Write the next part of the script.

1. Mom: Hi, Brian. How was school today?

   Brian: It was great. Wait until you hear about it. You are going to smile from ear to ear.

   Mom: I cannot wait to hear about your day. What happened?

   Brian: _____

   _____

   _____

2. Dad: Sean, are you awake?

   Sean: Wow, I am so tired! I almost fell asleep right here at the baseball game.

   Dad: Well, I am not surprised after last night.

   Sean: _____

   _____

   _____

3. Sandra: What time did Tina say that she would be here?

   Missy: She said that she would be here right after her soccer game. It should be any minute.

   Sandra: I wonder what her big surprise is. She said that it definitely involves us.

   Missy: She has been very sneaky lately, and I did hear her say something about a famous rock group.

   Tina: _____

   _____

   _____

Helping at Home

Have your child think of two well-known characters, such as Harry Potter and Laura Ingalls, and write a short dialogue for them. The characters' names should not be directly stated. Read your child's writing. Can you guess the two characters?

Writing a Story Ending

Good stories have good endings.

Read the story details. Write a satisfying ending to the story by asking a question or having the characters learn a lesson.

Characters
Scotty is a golden retriever who loves to play fetch.
Mark is Scotty's owner.

Problem
Scotty gets lost in the park while playing fetch with Mark.

Solution
Mark finally finds Scotty waiting for him by the swings.

Satisfying Ending

_____

_____

_____

_____

_____

_____

_____

_____

_____

_____

Helping at Home

Talk with your child about book or movie endings that you found unsatisfying. Ask your child to choose one idea and write an alternate ending for the story. Your child may wish to publish the ending anonymously on a book or movie review Web site.

Writing a Story

Write a story that tells about your favorite childhood memory. Include dialogue as you remember it. Use the flowchart to help you plan your story.

Setting: _____

Characters: _____

Problem: _____

Event 1: _____
_____
_____
_____
_____
_____
_____

Event 2: _____
_____
_____
_____
_____
_____
_____

Event 3: _____
_____
_____
_____
_____
_____
_____

Solution: _____

Using this information, write a five-sentence paragraph that tells about the story.

_____

_____

_____

Helping at Home

Share one of your own vivid childhood memories with your child. Encourage your child to ask you questions about the event, take notes, and write it as a story. In turn, you may wish to write a short story about one of your child's memories.

The Writing Process

Use the editing checklist to produce a final copy of your story from page 46. Type your final draft on the computer or write it on another sheet of paper.

Plan

_____ I have made a written plan that outlines the setting, characters, events, and conclusion of my story.

Revise

_____ I have written an interesting start to my story that catches the reader's attention.

_____ I have written a closing that effectively ends my story.

_____ I have revised my writing for vivid and descriptive words.

_____ I used transition words and phrases to connect my writing.

Edit

_____ I used words correctly.

_____ I have written complete sentences.

_____ I have edited my writing for correct capitalization and punctuation.

_____ I have edited my writing for spelling errors.

Publish

_____ I have decided how I will publish and share my writing.

Helping at Home
Read and admire your child's finished story. Suggest that he or she place it in a special decorated folder or binder to be kept on your family's bookshelf. Over time, add more of your child's writing.

Relative Pronouns and Adverbs

Fill in the blanks using relative pronouns from the word bank.

that	whichever	whoever	whomever
which	who	whom	whose

1. This is the new bicycle _____ I bought with my allowance.

2. The drama coach chose students _____ he thought were the best actors.

3. I want to ride with _____ is the best driver.

4. _____ student got the best grades would pass out the awards.

5. _____ finishes their dinner can have dessert.

6. My neighbor, _____ cat won't come down, is understandably upset.

7. The pot roast, _____ was left out overnight, should be thrown out.

8. The person _____ has the latest birthday will go first.

Fill in the blank using a relative adverb from the word bank. One of them will be used twice.

where	when	why

9. That is the school _____ I first met you.

10. It was a very hot day _____ Jose went swimming for the first time.

11. Tell me _____ you can't make it for practice.

12. Kelly will hand it in _____ she has answered all the questions.

Helping at Home

The pronouns *who* and *whom* are often confused. *Who* refers to the subject of a sentence while *whom* refers to the object. Teach your child a trick: If the word can be replaced by *he*, it should be *who*. If it can be replaced by *him*, it should be *whom*.

Verb Tenses

Write the progressive tense of each verb. **Example:** *was walking, am walking, will be walking*

	past progressive	present progressive	future progressive
1. write	_____	_____	_____
2. swim	_____	_____	_____
3. read	_____	_____	_____
4. play	_____	_____	_____
5. eat	_____	_____	_____
6. sit	_____	_____	_____

Complete each sentence with the correct progressive tense of each verb in parentheses.

7. I _____ soccer after school right now. (play)

8. Next fall, I _____ a different sport. (play)

9. In first grade, I _____ much easier sports. (play)

Circle the best modal auxiliary verb to complete the sentence.

10. I (can, could) play "Old MacDonald" on the piano already.

11. The senator (may, might) become president in two years.

12. She (must, has to) clean her room before she can go to the mall.

13. I (shall, should) eat a salad for lunch.

14. The team (will, would) always win the game when they played well.

Helping at Home Have your child search for and read the poem "Fog" by Carl Sandburg. How many ways can your child write the first line—*The fog comes on little cat feet*—using different verb tenses, including progressive verb tenses?

Complete Sentences

Use the nouns and verbs to write sentences with complete subjects and complete predicates.

1. car   roar

_____

2. birds   flock

_____

3. helmets   ride

_____

4. students   run

_____

5. glasses   break

_____

Draw a box around each complete subject. Circle each complete predicate. Underline any sentence fragments. Rewrite each fragment as a complete sentence.

6. The gentle manatee lives in shallow water. _____

7. Sometimes called sea cows. _____

8. Most West Indian manatees live in Florida. _____

9. They look for food at the water's surface. _____

10. A resting manatee. _____

11. The average adult manatee is three meters (9.8 feet) long. _____

12. Manatees eat all types of plants. _____

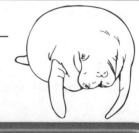

Many students have trouble recognizing sentence fragments, which lack a subject or verb (example: *found it here*), and run-on sentences with double subjects and verbs (example: *we looked everywhere we found it here*). Help your child find and correct examples in his or her writing.

Helping at Home

Adjectives, Prepositional Phrases, and Homophones

Write the pair of adjectives in the correct order.

1. The dog is a _____, _____ Labrador retriever. (black, big)

2. I am going to bake a _____, _____ cake. (chocolate, delicious)

3. Please recycle the _____, _____ water bottles. (empty, six)

4. Robert is wearing a _____, _____ coat. (green, long)

5. She gave Tanisha some _____, _____ clothes. (pretty, new)

Underline the prepositional phrase in each sentence.

6. The dime fell between the cracks.

7. The money for my lunch is missing.

8. Juan fell on the steps and hurt himself.

9. Miss Gomez was visiting our school from a nearby college.

10. Mrs. Chang wrote a note about my behavior.

Choose the correct word from the list to complete each sentence.

11. _____ going to be the best one of _____ kind. (it's, its)

12. I stopped _____ the store to _____ some milk. (by, buy)

13. The _____ beat the tortoise by a _____. (hair, hare)

14. Marta went _____ the store today. Abby was there _____.

    So, the _____ girls shopped together. (to, too, two)

15. I heard _____ are going to be at least 100 people at _____

    wedding. My neighbors said that _____ going to be there, too. (there, they're, their)

Helping at Home
The homophones *its* and *it's* and *there*, *their*, and *they're* are frequently confused. Have your child create a worksheet or word puzzle that provides practice for using each word correctly and share it with his or her teacher to use at school.

Capitalization and Punctuation

Rewrite these sentences. Add quotation marks, capitalization, and punctuation where needed.

1. can we please stay for 10 more minutes the children asked

_____

2. i knew about the surprise party all along jonah admitted

_____

3. that was a really silly joke alyssa giggled

_____

4. I think i have a cold so dont get too close maggie warned

_____

5. shh she might hear us liz whispered

_____

6. i didnt mean to do it but I couldn't help myself serena confessed

_____

7. you can do it the coach cheered

_____

8. first line up all of the numbers and then add them the teacher explained.

_____

9. the water in the pool is chilly today the lifeguard warned

_____

10. stir the ingredients well the cooking instructor suggested

_____

Send your child a one-sentence e-mail or text message that is missing several capital letters and punctuation marks. Have your child correct the message and send it back to you. Keep trading messages to proofread and return.

Using Quotation Marks

Rewrite the sentences. Add quotations marks and capital letters where needed.

1. i thought about taking a bus, but I finally decided to take an airplane, Emily said.

_____

_____

2. i am not sure, tony sighed. i just can't remember where i left my keys. _____

_____

_____

3. the treasure is hidden in the forest, the prince whispered. _____

_____

4. did you see where melinda went? tyler asked. i want to invite her over for lunch.

_____

_____

5. sue asked, do you know how to grow an herb garden? _____

_____

6. i want to learn to play the cello, maria said. will you teach me? _____

_____

7. jelly beans are my favorite! Daniel shouted. i love the cherry-flavored ones.

_____

_____

Helping at Home

Have your child choose a funny or memorable scene from a recorded movie, video, or TV show. Ask your child to write each line from the scene, pausing as needed to catch all the words. Remind your child to use quotation marks correctly.

Spelling

Read the story. Cross out each word that is misspelled. Then, write the correct spellings on the lines below. Use a dictionary if you need it.

Stained Glass

Alexis and Emma had to write a report for werld history. They were studying the Middle Ages. Some of the boys were writing reports about nights, the Black Death, and the Krusades. Some of the girls were writing reports about tapestries, costumes, and liturature.

Alexis and Emma wanted to do something different. They met one Saturday at the library. They used the catolog on the computer to find books about the Middle Ages.

They found many subjects listed under Middle Ages. Alexis pointed to Gothic Cathedral. "Just last month, I saw a documentary about building a cathedral," she said. "Everybody in the town helped. Some men started working on the cathedral when they were yung. They worked on it their whole lives."

"That was a book too," said Emma. "I read it last year. Let's find the books on cathedrals."

The two girls printed out the list of books. Then, they found the write sektion in the library. Two of the books were checked out, but the other for were on the shelf. Alexis took two, and Emma took two.

They went to a quiet table and started to look at the pictures. Alexis found a picture of a beutiful stained glass window.

She read that the cathedrals were made of stone. They were also very tall. They needed big windows to bring light into the building. The artists desined windows made of pieces of colorful glass. When light came through the windows, people inside the cathedral could see glowing pictures or designs.

Alexis showed Emma the picture. They decided to write their report on staned glass windows in cathedrals.

1. _____
2. _____
3. _____
4. _____
5. _____
6. _____
7. _____
8. _____
9. _____
10. _____
11. _____
12. _____

Helping at Home

Provide a little notebook where your child can keep an alphabetized list of "spelling demons," or words that are especially difficult to spell correctly. He or she might begin with these tricky words: *cupboard, often, receive, straight, tomorrow.*

Word Choice

Write a sentence to convey the emotion in parentheses.

1. (happiness) _____

_____

2. (excitement) _____

_____

3. (sorrow) _____

_____

4. (disappointment) _____

_____

5. (surprise) _____

_____

Look at each pair of sentences. Place an **S** for *slang* or a **P** for *proper English* in front of each.

6. _____ Let's call it a day, man.

_____ Let's stop working now.

7. _____ That race was quite easy for me.

_____ That race was a piece of cake, bro.

8. _____ Hang in there.

_____ Keep trying.

9. _____ Tell my friends I said hello.

_____ Say hey to my peeps for me.

10. _____ C'mon, take a load off.

_____ Take it easy.

Helping at Home

Role-play with your child situations in which it is acceptable to use slang and situations that require formal speech. How would your child request something from a friend? How would he or she request something from the principal?

Ending Punctuation

Put a question mark at the end of each interrogative sentence. Put an exclamation point at the end of each exclamatory sentence.

1. Do you know how many teeth an adult human has

2. Does he or she have 32 teeth

3. Did you realize that zebras have teeth like rats

4. Hey! You must be kidding

5. Wow! Zebras grind down their teeth by eating 15 hours a day

6. Can their teeth just keep growing like rodents' teeth

7. That is amazing

8. Is it true that great white sharks have razor-sharp teeth

Rewrite each sentence and add the correct ending punctuation mark. Then, read the sentences aloud to another person with the proper emphasis.

9. You will not believe this

_____

10. What are you talking about

_____

11. Wow! A snail has teeth on its tongue

_____

12. Goodness! There are thousands of tiny teeth

_____

Helping at Home

Ask your child to look up *interrogative* and *exclamation* in the dictionary. How do their meanings relate to the types of sentences they describe? Have your child draw the words in the shape of a question mark and exclamation point, respectively.

Context Clues

Read the story.

King Arthur

Legend says that England once had a **noble** king named Arthur who fought for good and **respectable** things. There are many stories from the Middle Ages in which King Arthur is the hero. He **defeated** his foes and won the love and admiration of his countrymen.

King Arthur held his court in a place called Camelot, and his knights sat at a round table. The symbolic round table showed that they all worked together and that no one was at the head of the table. In King Arthur's court, no knight had more responsibility or **influence** than any other knight. King Arthur is said to have brought order and peace to his kingdom.

As a child, Arthur discovered his **regal** legacy when he was the only person who could free a sword that was **lodged** in a stone outside a cathedral. Arthur's father and mother died when he was young, and he was raised by his uncle.

With the help of a magician, Merlin, he was guided to his destiny. He later married the beautiful Guinevere, whom he loved deeply. He and his knights were known for their kindness, gentleness, and chivalry. He received his famous sword, Excalibur, as a gift from the "Lady of the Lake." This was the sword that he used in battle many times. Some **legends** say that King Arthur died on the Isle of Avalon. Others say that Arthur will return one day.

Based on the context of each bold word, write a brief definition.

1. _____

2. _____

3. _____

4. _____

5. _____

6. _____

7. _____

Helping at Home Encourage your child to read a newspaper or nonfiction article with challenging vocabulary. Have your child choose one unfamiliar word in the piece. Together, look for context clues that help define the word.

Word Parts

Draw lines to match the prefix with its meaning, then another line to an example. Use a dictionary for help if you need it.

1. anti-	A. before	a. bicycle
2. bi-	B. after	b. introduction
3. intro-	C. half	c. semicircle
4. micro-	D. against	d. multicultural
5. multi-	E. many	e. nonreader
6. non-	F. three	f. antibiotic
7. post-	G. not	g. microchip
8. pre-	H. again	h. previous
9. re-	I. small	i. unnecessary
10. semi-	J. two	j. recreate
11. tri-	K. inward	k. postwar
12. un-	L. not	l. tricycle

Helping at Home

Choose five prefixes from this page. Challenge your child to think of another example of a word that includes each prefix or do some research to find one. How does the meaning of the example word relate to the meaning of the prefix?

Similes and Metaphors

Complete each simile.

1. as stubborn as _____

2. as clumsy as _____

3. as loud as _____

Write a sentence using each simile that you created.

4. _____

5. _____

6. _____

Read the metaphors. Write a sentence explaining the meaning of each metaphor.

Example: He clammed up when his parents asked him who broke the vase.
This means that he kept his mouth closed when his parents questioned him.

7. The stars were jewels in the night sky. _____

_____

8. Jessica is a treasure chest of ideas. _____

_____

9. My mind was a sponge soaking up all of her brilliant ideas. _____

_____

10. The field wore a coat of gold. _____

_____

Helping at Home

Have your child search online for an image of *The Flower Carrier* by artist Diego Rivera. Ask your child what he or she notices about the painting. Then, have your child write one simile and one metaphor to describe it.

Idioms

Read the idioms. Explain what you think each one means.

1. Piece of cake: _____

2. Tongue-tied: _____

3. Over-the-hill: _____

4. Hit the sack: _____

5. All ears: _____

Write a sentence using each idiom.

6. Cat got your tongue: _____

_____

7. See eye to eye: _____

_____

8. Toot your own horn: _____

_____

9. Raining cats and dogs: _____

_____

10. A piece of cake: _____

_____

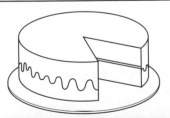

Helping at Home

Have your child research other common idiomatic expressions in English and choose a favorite. It could be *a penny for your thoughts* or *missed the boat*. Ask your child to illustrate the literal and figurative meanings of the expression.

Figurative Language

Identify whether each sentence includes a simile or a metaphor. Write **S** if the sentence includes a simile. Write **M** is the sentence includes a metaphor.

1. _____ The ocean is a hungry animal.

2. _____ Her expression was as sour as a lime.

3. _____ I dried the dishes so well that they sparkled like diamonds.

4. _____ My room is a junkyard.

5. _____ Gavin's compliment made my face turn red as an apple.

Describe your best friend. Write one sentence using a simile and one sentence using a metaphor.

6. Simile: _____

7. Metaphor: _____

These statements contain idioms. Read the sentences. Circle the answers that give the correct meanings of the idioms.

8. Alice had butterflies in her stomach before the tennis match.

    A. was coming down with the flu   B. was nervous

9. Tell me about it. I'm all ears.

    A. listening carefully   B. covered in ears

10. That noise is driving me up the wall.

    A. bothering me   B. very loud

Helping at Home

Look for the books *There's a Frog in My Throat* by Loreen Leedy and *Parts, More Parts,* and *Even More Parts* by Tedd Arnold. These silly books are all about idioms and the funny misunderstandings that can result when they are taken literally.

Synonyms and Antonyms

Write the word that is the antonym of the other words. Use a dictionary if needed.

1. young   early   old   juvenile _____

2. cold   hot   chilly   freezing _____

3. dirty   clean   sterile   immaculate _____

4. flop   fail   win   lose _____

5. fling   throw   toss   catch _____

6. sluggish   fast   slow   leisurely _____

7. grand   impressive   magnificent   humble _____

8. neat   orderly   sloppy   tidy _____

Circle the synonym in parentheses for each bold word in the sentences.

9. My mother was surprised when she saw the **beautiful** flowers. (pretty, red)

10. The librarian asked Maria to be **silent** because her classmates were trying to study. (cheerful, quiet)

11. My brother rode a **miniature** pony on his birthday. (pretty, small)

12. The judge made a **wise** decision about the case. (funny, intelligent)

13. Sam's grandfather is too **elderly** to walk that far. (old, interesting)

14. Adele's parents will enjoy their 20th anniversary **celebration**. (party, parade)

15. Aren't you **exhausted** after your long race? (hungry, tired)

16. Algebra problems are **difficult** for many kids. (hard, easy)

Have your child brainstorm a list of overused words such as *nice*, *good*, *fun*, and *cool*. "Catch" your child using these words and ask him or her to substitute a synonym such as *marvelous* or *fascinating*. Let your child "catch" you using overused words, too.

Word Meanings

Imagine a beetle so bright that humans used it instead of a candle at night. The cucujo beetle found in Central America is that bug. Native people long ago would tie cucujos to their feet to light their way along steep mountain paths. During summer festivals, young girls would decorate their hair with this glowing beetle.

The light is produced from a chemical reaction called **bioluminescence** (bi/o/loom/in/es/since). There are insects, fish, and even some plants that produce this light.

Fireflies, or lightning bugs, are found in the eastern United States. (Fireflies are not actually flies. They're beetles.) They are seen on warm evenings in early summer. This beetle is the only insect that can flash its light on and off. The male flashes a pattern of light to females resting on the ground. Think of it as the firefly's way of asking for a date. Sometimes frogs eat so many fireflies that they start to glow from the inside out.

In the Pacific and Indian Oceans and the Red Sea, flashlight fish live among coral reefs. As the sun sets, they rise to the surface. Smaller fish attracted by the light become easy **prey**. There is no creature that gives off a brighter light. In fact, fishermen can see the light over 100 feet away!

The light is caused by **bacteria**. The bacteria grow in patches below the fish's eyes and give off a blue-green glow. When trying to avoid a **predator**, the flashlight fish constantly changes directions as it swims away. To confuse its attacker, it blinks its light on and off. It does this by slipping a cover, like an eyelid, over the shining patches.

Other night creatures that glow in the dark are anchovies, jellyfish, squid, some earthworms, and the railroad worm. A fungus or mushroom called the yellow jack-o'-lantern produces a bright greenish light. But don't eat it—it's **poisonous**.

Use each word in a sentence. Consult a dictionary if you need help.

1. bioluminescence _____

2. prey _____

3. bacteria _____

4. predator _____

5. poisonous _____

Provide a notebook where your child can keep lists of words and definitions related to school subject areas or topics of interest. For example, if your child is interested in ocean animals, he or she might list *marine, mollusk, plankton,* or *reef.*

Common Core State Standards for Math*

The following parent-friendly explanations of fourth grade Common Core math standards are provided to help you understand what your child will learn in school this year. Practice pages listed will help your child master each skill.

Complete Common Core State Standards may be found here: www.corestandards.org.

4.OA Operations and Algebraic Thinking

Use the four operations with whole numbers to solve problems.
(Standards: 4.OA.A.1, 4.OA.A.2, 4.OA.A.3)

Your child will understand multiplication equations as comparisons. For example, he or she will notice that 35 is five times as many as seven and seven times as many as five.
• **Practice pages: 68–71**

Your child will solve multi-step word problems that involve addition, subtraction, multiplication, and division. • **Practice pages: 72, 73**

Gain familiarity with factors and multiples.
(Standard: 4.OA.B.4)

Your child will learn about factors, or numbers that can be multiplied to get a certain number. For example, these numbers are factors of 24: 1, 2, 3, 4, 6, 8, 12, 24. • **Practice pages: 74, 75**

Generate and analyze patterns.
(Standard: 4.OA.C.5)

Your child will work with number patterns and determine the rule that governs a pattern. For example, this pattern illustrates the rule "multiply by 2": 8, 16, 32, 64. • **Practice pages: 76, 77**

4.NBT Number and Operations in Base Ten

Generalize place value understanding for multi-digit whole numbers.
(Standards: 4.NBT.A.1, 4.NBT.A.2, 4.NBT.A.3)

Your child will work with multi-digit numbers and write them in expanded form. For example, 2,868 is the same as two thousand eight hundred sixty-eight. Your child will use an understanding of place value to compare two large numbers and tell which is greater or less.
• **Practice pages: 78, 79**

Your child will use an understanding of place value to round large, multi-digit numbers to any place. For example, 589,712 rounded to the nearest ten thousand is 590,000.
• **Practice pages: 80, 81**

Use place value understanding and properties of operations to perform multi-digit arithmetic.
(Standards: 4.NBT.B.4, 4.NBT.B.5, 4.NBT.B.6)

Your child will add and subtract large, multi-digit numbers. • **Practice pages: 82, 83**

Your child will multiply a multi-digit number by a one-digit number and multiply two two-digit numbers. • **Practice pages: 84–86**

Your child will divide multi-digit numbers by one-digit numbers to find answers (or quotients) that may have remainders. • **Practice pages: 87–89**

4.NF Number and Operations–Fractions

Extend understanding of fraction equivalence and ordering.
(Standards: 4.NF.A.1, 4.NF.A.2)

Your child will look at visual models of fractions and understand that two different fractions are equal because they name the same part of a whole. He or she will form and write equivalent fractions. For example, $\frac{3}{6}$ and $\frac{4}{8}$ are equivalent fractions because they both name $\frac{1}{2}$ of a whole. • **Practice pages: 90, 91**

Your child will compare two fractions with different numerators and denominators and tell which is greater or less. • **Practice pages: 93, 94**

Build fractions from unit fractions by applying and extending previous understandings of operations on whole numbers.
(Standards: 4.NF.B.3a, 4.NF.B.3b, 4.NF.B.3c, 4.NF.B.3d,
4.NF.B.4a, 4.NF.B.4b, 4.NF.B.4c)

Your child will add and subtract fractions with like denominators. • **Practice pages: 95–97**

Your child will work with improper fractions (such as $\frac{5}{3}$) and mixed numbers (such as $1\frac{2}{3}$) and understand that $1\frac{2}{3}$ is the same as $\frac{3}{3} + \frac{1}{3} + \frac{1}{3}$. He or she will add and subtract mixed numbers with like denominators. • **Practice pages: 98–100**

Common Core State Standards for Math*

Your child will multiply fractions by whole numbers. • **Practice pages: 101, 102**

Understand decimal notation for fractions, and compare decimal fractions.
(Standards: 4.NF.C.5, 4.NF.C.6, 4.NF.C.7)

Your child will use an understanding of place value to add fractions with denominators of 10 and 100. For example, he or she will solve $\frac{7}{10} + \frac{3}{100}$ by changing $\frac{7}{10}$ to $\frac{70}{100}$ and adding $\frac{70}{100} + \frac{3}{100}$.
• **Practice page: 92**

Your child will learn how to use decimals to express fractions with denominators of 10 or 100. For example, he or she will change $\frac{74}{100}$ to .74. • **Practice pages: 103–105**

Your child will compare two decimal numbers to the hundredths place to tell which is greater or less. • **Practice pages: 106, 107**

4.MD Measurement and Data

Solve problems involving measurement and conversion of measurements from a larger unit to a smaller unit.
(Standards: 4.MD.A.1, 4.MD.A.2, 4.MD.A.3)

Your child will convert measurements from larger units to smaller units. For example, he or she will determine that there are 36 inches in one yard or 1,000 milliliters in one liter.
• **Practice pages: 108, 109**

Your child will use addition, subtraction, multiplication, and division to solve word problems about distance, time, volume, weight, and money. • **Practice pages: 110, 111**

Your child will learn to use the standard formulas for finding the perimeter and area of rectangular shapes. • **Practice pages: 112, 113**

Represent and interpret data.
(Standard: 4.MD.B.4)

Your child will measure things in fractions of units (for example, $\frac{1}{4}$ inch, $\frac{1}{2}$ inch, etc.) and record the data using a line plot. • **Practice page: 114**

Geometric measurement: understand concepts of angle and measure angles.
(Standards: 4.MD.C.5, 4.MD.C.6, 4.MD.C.7)

Your child will study angles and measure angles in degrees. • **Practice pages: 115, 116**

Your child will add the measurements of non-overlapping angles. For example, 45° + 45° = 90°. • **Practice page: 117**

4.G Geometry

Draw and identify lines and angles, and classify shapes by properties
of their lines and angles.
(Standards: 4.G.A.1, 4.G.A.2, 4.G.A.3)

Your child will learn to identify points, lines, line segments, rays, angles, perpendicular lines, and parallel lines. • **Practice pages: 115, 116, 118, 119**

Your child will learn to look for parallel lines, perpendicular lines, and angles in two-dimensional shapes such as rectangles and triangles. • **Practice page: 120**

Your child will look for symmetry in shapes and draw lines of symmetry when shapes can be folded down the middle into matching parts. • **Practice page: 121**

Understanding Multiplication

Use the numbers to complete two true sentences for each fact family.

1. 7, 6, 42 _____ is _____ times as many as _____. _____ is _____ times as many as _____.	2. 2, 4, 8 _____ is _____ times as many as _____. _____ is _____ times as many as _____.
3. 5, 8, 40 _____ is _____ times as many as _____. _____ is _____ times as many as _____.	4. 3, 7, 21 _____ is _____ times as many as _____. _____ is _____ times as many as _____.
5. 9, 4, 36 _____ is _____ times as many as _____. _____ is _____ times as many as _____.	6. 12, 6, 72 _____ is _____ times as many as _____. _____ is _____ times as many as _____.
7. 3, 9, 27 _____ is _____ times as many as _____. _____ is _____ times as many as _____.	8. 4, 5, 20 _____ is _____ times as many as _____. _____ is _____ times as many as _____.

Helping at Home

Challenge your child to write a division problem using the numbers from the fact family in each item on this page.

Understanding Multiplication

Write an equation to match each sentence. Find the answer to each equation in the bunch of balloons, and color it the matching color.

1. eight times as many as six (red)	2. seven times as many as four (blue)
3. twelve times as many as seven (green)	4. five times as many as eleven (yellow)
5. six times as many as nine (purple)	6. nine times as many as eight (orange)
7. nine times as many as three (light green)	8. seven times as many as nine (pink)

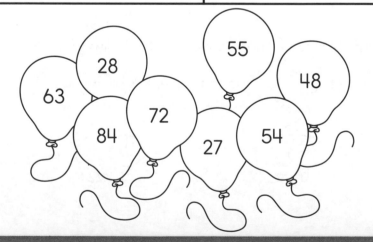

Helping at Home

Give your child a number such as *48, 96,* or *100*. How many different multiplication problems can he or she think of that have that number as a product? Have your child give you numbers, too.

Word Problems

Complete the equation for each word problem. Then, find the value of the symbol.

1. There are 5 times as many frogs in Green Lake as there are in Blue Lake. If there are 25 frogs in Green Lake, how many are in Blue Lake? Let 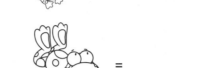 stand for the number of frogs in Blue Lake.

   25 ÷ _____ = 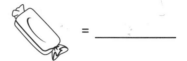   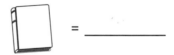 = _____

2. Jordan has 8 times as many candies as Jessica. If Jordan has 24 candies, how many does Jessica have? Let 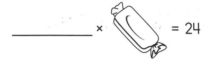 stand for the number of candies Jessica has.

   _____ × 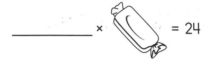 = 24   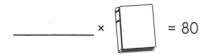 = _____

3. Julio read 10 times as many pages as Carlos. If Julio read 80 pages, how many did Carlos read? Let ▯ stand for the number of pages Carlos has read.

   _____ × ▯ = 80   ▯ = _____

4. Madison gets 3 times the allowance that Derek gets. If Madison gets $15 per week, how much money does Derek get? Let 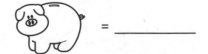 stand for Derek's allowance.

   _____ ÷ _____ =    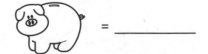 = _____

Word Problems

Draw a picture to represent each scenario. Then, write the fact that answers the question. The first one is done for you.

1. Michael has 3 times as many clovers as Danielle. Danielle has 12 clovers.

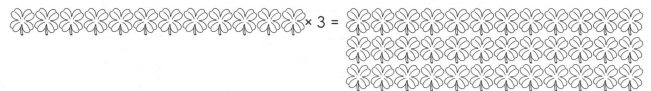 × 3 =

 $12 \times 3 = 36$

2. Justin has 5 times as many baseball cards as David. David has 6 cards.

3. Olivia has 16 pairs of shoes, which is twice as many as Claire.

4. Chang has 8 times as many coins as Dave. Dave has 4 coins.

5. Melanie has 21 rocks, which is 3 times as many as Jamie.

Helping at Home Ask your child to research the cost of a new game or article of clothing and round it to the nearest whole number. How much would three of the items cost? Ten of the items? Have your child draw pictures to show the answers.

Multi-Step Problems

Read through the story to find out how many tickets each child has. Then, fill in the blank underneath each child to show his or her total number of tickets.

As a way to earn rewards, the students in Ms. Lindbergh's 4th grade class earn tickets for positive behavior. Elizabeth has 82 tickets, which is more than anyone else in the class. Jacob is trailing Elizabeth by 9 tickets, and Jacob has 1 more ticket than Eric. Eric has 9 times as many tickets as George but 5 fewer tickets than Emily. Claire has 3 times as many tickets as George but half as many tickets as Demetri.

Elizabeth

_____

Jacob

_____

Eric

_____

George

_____

Emily

_____

Claire

_____

Demetri

_____

Imagine that the students in Ms. Lindbergh's class can spend 6 of their tickets on a prize from the prize box. How many prizes could each student get? How many tickets would each student have left over after getting a prize?

Multi-Step Problems

Solve each problem.

1. Elizabeth had a box of 24 crayons. Her little brother ate 2 of them, and she lost 4 of them. She split the remaining crayons between her and her 2 friends. How many crayons did each friend get?

2. Carlos's mom gave him $10 for lunch. He spent $4 on his lunch and $2 on an ice cream cone, and he found $3 on the playground. How much money does Carlos have now?

3. Mrs. Chu had 20 books on the shelf in her room. The principal gave her 3 times as many to add to her shelf, and she donated 10 to the 3rd grade room. How many books does Mrs. Chu have on her shelf now?

4. Noah has a bag of jelly beans to share with his friends. The bag contains 57 jelly beans, and Noah wants to share them with 6 people. He plans to give the leftovers to his little brother. In order to split the jelly beans evenly, how many will he need to give to his brother?

Helping at Home

After your child completes this page, ask him or her to choose one item and make a list of each operation used (addition, subtraction, multiplication, and division) to solve the problem.

Factors and Multiples

Shade the squares in the grid containing the factors of each number.

1. 56 (yellow)   2. 99 (green)

3. 72 (orange)   4. 50 (blue)

1	2	3	4	5	6	7	8	9	10
11	12	13	14	15	16	17	18	19	20
21	22	23	24	25	26	27	28	29	30
31	32	33	34	35	36	37	38	39	40
41	42	43	44	45	46	47	48	49	50
51	52	53	54	55	56	57	58	59	60
61	62	63	64	65	66	67	68	69	70
71	72	73	74	75	76	77	78	79	80
81	82	83	84	85	86	87	88	89	90
91	92	93	94	95	96	97	98	99	100

Helping at Home

Challenge your child to list numbers from the chart that are prime, with no factors other than 1 and themselves. Which numbers have one factor, two factors, three factors, etc.?

Factors and Multiples

In each row, cross out the factor that does not belong to the number.

Number	Factor				
1. 18	6	9	4	2	3
2. 20	10	4	2	6	5
3. 36	4	12	18	16	3
4. 52	13	21	4	2	26
5. 72	24	7	9	12	6
6. 12	1	5	3	4	6
7. 24	3	7	8	4	6
8. 50	20	2	25	50	5
9. 64	16	3	4	8	2
10. 80	5	16	8	9	20

Factor each number.

11. 30

12. 25

13. 40

14. 32

Give your child clues to a number. For the number 24, you might say that it has factors of 2 and 4, that it has two digits, and that the product of its two digits is 8. Can your child guess the number? Have your child give you clues, too.

Patterns

Write a rule that fits the description of each pattern. Give the first five numbers or shapes for each pattern.

1. starts at 3 and alternates between even and odd numbers without adding one

2. starts at 100, uses division, and the numbers are always even

3. starts at 3, uses multiplication, and the numbers are always odd

4. shape pattern starting with 1 block and the figure must remain square

5. starts at 2 and uses multiplication

6. shape pattern starting with 3 blocks

7. starts at 82 and uses subtraction

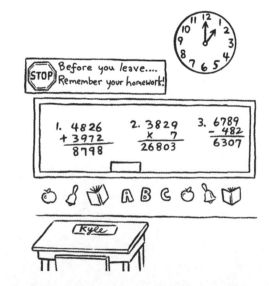

Helping at Home Challenge your child to make a pattern of numbers and show it to you. Can you determine the rule that governs the pattern? Can you add the next number to the pattern? Make patterns for your child to solve, too.

Patterns

Write the next 3 numbers and the rule for each pattern.

1. 1, 2, 4, 7, 11, 16, 22, _____, _____, _____

    Rule: _____

2. 81, 76, 71, 66, 61, 56, 51, _____, _____, _____

    Rule: _____

3. 1, 1, 2, 2, 4, 4, 8, 8, _____, _____, _____

    Rule: _____

4. 6, 12, 22, 44, 54, 108, 118, _____, _____, _____

    Rule: _____

5. 100, 99, 97, 94, 90, 85, _____, _____, _____

    Rule: _____

6. 1, 4, 8, 11, 22, 25, _____, _____, _____

    Rule: _____

7. 5, 4, 10, 9, 15, 14, 20, _____, _____, _____

    Rule: _____

8. 9, 27, 17, 51, 41, 123, 113, _____, _____, _____

    Rule: _____

9. $\frac{1}{2}$, $\frac{5}{8}$, $\frac{3}{4}$, $\frac{7}{8}$, 1, $\frac{9}{8}$, _____, _____, _____

    Rule: _____

10. 40, 8, 80, 16, 160, 32, 320, _____, _____, _____

    Rule: _____

© Carson-Dellosa • CD-704504

Helping at Home

Ask your child to choose one item from this page. Can he or she keep going with the pattern, extending it until it includes 100 numbers? Numbers can be added to the front or the back of the pattern to extend it.

Place Value

Write each number in expanded form.

1. 77

2. 357

3. 2,560

4. 459

5. 3,912

6. 1,003

Write each number in expanded form. Then, explain the relationship between the number in the ones place, the tens place, and the hundreds place.

7. 88

8. 555

9. 33

10. 222

© Carson-Dellosa • CD-704504

Helping at Home Challenge your child to write a very large number (with six or more digits) on a large sheet of paper. Can he or she write the place name (ones, tens, hundreds, thousands, ten thousands, etc.) below each digit in the number?

Comparing Numbers

Write >, <, or = to compare each pair of numbers.

1. 24,064 ( ) 27,590

2. 56,000 ( ) 56,000

3. 2,641 ( ) 3,461

4. 17,048 ( ) 15,084

5. 22,728 ( ) 22,782

6. 55,491 ( ) 55,941

7. 8,463 ( ) 6,891

8. 85,485 ( ) 89,849

9. 74,912 ( ) 43,819

10. 83,214 ( ) 83,214

11. 54,295 ( ) 82,918

12. 924,146 ( ) 948,962

Order each set of numbers from least to greatest.

13. 1,408,241   9,426,597   1,400,892

_____

14. 342,192   328,191   340,384

_____

15. 68,297   405,495   929,058   65,382

_____

16. 385,722   456,817   395,024   409,990

_____

Helping at Home

Think aloud as you help your child complete one item on this page.
For #1, say, "First, look at the ten thousands place. Those digits
are the same, so look at the thousands place. 27,000 is more than
24,000, so the second number is greater."

Rounding Multi-Digit Numbers

Round the amount in each treasure chest to the nearest hundred.

1.

$692

$ _____

2.

$140

$ _____

3.

$569

$ _____

4.

$3,703

$ _____

5.

$1,684

$ _____

6.

$851

$ _____

7.

$1,456,823

$ _____

8.

$345,231

$ _____

9.

$249,999

$ _____

Rounding Multi-Digit Numbers

Round to the nearest ten.

1. 72 _____

2. 55 _____

3. 14 _____

4. 62 _____

5. 83 _____

6. 17 _____

7. 49 _____

8. 29 _____

Round to the nearest hundred.

9. 284 _____

10. 924 _____

11. 561 _____

12. 354 _____

13. 752 _____

14. 728 _____

15. 689 _____

16. 192 _____

Round to the nearest thousand.

17. 1,432 _____

18. 2,418 _____

19. 1,242 _____

20. 4,299 _____

21. 6,419 _____

22. 7,546 _____

23. 9,721 _____

24. 4,142 _____

25. 5,948 _____

Round to the nearest ten thousand.

26. 23,56 _____

27. 97,453 _____

28. 12,971 _____

Round to the nearest hundred thousand.

29. 238,249 _____

30. 956,235 _____

31. 200,345 _____

Helping at Home

After your child completes this page, ask him or her to choose five of the items and use a highlighter pen to mark the digit in each number that was used to decide if the number should be rounded up or down.

Addition and Subtraction

Add or subtract.

1. 344
    + 251

2. 467
    + 139

3. 267
    + 149

4. 3,787
    + 147

5. 6,971
    + 534

6. 2,748
    + 2,147

7. 5,471
    + 2,787

8. 4,387
    + 1,349

9. 3,661
    + 2,677

10. 28,920
    + 6,378

11. 74
    67
    + 36

12. 74
    71
    + 13

13. 73
    46
    + 27

14. 272
    156
    + 38

15. 7,514
    6,372
    + 5,401

16. 437
    24
    21
    + 13

17. 680
    71
    63
    + 14

18. 304
    41
    33
    + 17

19. 674
    341
    231
    + 143

20. 6,324
    3,641
    3,541
    + 1,032

21. 653
    − 241

22. 364
    − 192

23. 467
    − 284

24. 613
    − 267

25. 504
    − 283

Helping at Home Provide a calendar. Ask your child to use addition and subtraction to answer these questions: How many days have passed in this month or year? How many days are still to come in this month or year? How many days until your birthday?

Word Problems

Solve each problem.

1. Stuart counted 5,671 red ants. Alice counted 6,105 black ants. How many more black ants than red ants were counted?

2. The Pets-R-Us pet store sold 733 pounds of birdseed in January. In February, the store sold 559 pounds of birdseed. How many pounds of birdseed did the store sell altogether?

3. The robin flew 3,419 feet. The blue jay flew 2,866 feet. How many more feet did the robin fly than the blue jay?

4. At the butterfly exhibit, Ryan saw 219 orange butterflies and 859 yellow butterflies. How many butterflies did Ryan see altogether?

5. There were 23,416 leafcutter ants in the rain forest. There were 16,980 beetles and 5,688 dragonflies. How many insects were there altogether?

6. In November, 9,717 birds flew south for the winter. Another 459 birds flew south in December. How many birds flew south altogether?

7. The garden contains 256 grasshoppers. If the garden contains 2,041 insects, how many insects are not grasshoppers?

8. Leslie saw 108 monarch butterflies in the field. Mario saw 849 monarch butterflies in the meadow. How many monarch butterflies did Leslie and Mario see altogether?

Helping at Home

After your child completes this page, ask him or her to highlight or underline words and phrases that signal whether to use addition or subtraction to solve the problem. For example, in item #6, the word *altogether* signals that addition should be used.

Multiplication

Multiply.

1. $\begin{array}{r} 21 \\ \times 5 \\ \hline \end{array}$	2. $\begin{array}{r} 32 \\ \times 3 \\ \hline \end{array}$	3. $\begin{array}{r} 11 \\ \times 8 \\ \hline \end{array}$	4. $\begin{array}{r} 41 \\ \times 2 \\ \hline \end{array}$	5. $\begin{array}{r} 13 \\ \times 2 \\ \hline \end{array}$	6. $\begin{array}{r} 34 \\ \times 2 \\ \hline \end{array}$
7. $\begin{array}{r} 19 \\ \times 2 \\ \hline \end{array}$	8. $\begin{array}{r} 24 \\ \times 3 \\ \hline \end{array}$	9. $\begin{array}{r} 35 \\ \times 2 \\ \hline \end{array}$	10. $\begin{array}{r} 47 \\ \times 2 \\ \hline \end{array}$	11. $\begin{array}{r} 36 \\ \times 4 \\ \hline \end{array}$	12. $\begin{array}{r} 27 \\ \times 4 \\ \hline \end{array}$
13. $\begin{array}{r} 54 \\ \times 4 \\ \hline \end{array}$	14. $\begin{array}{r} 27 \\ \times 6 \\ \hline \end{array}$	15. $\begin{array}{r} 19 \\ \times 6 \\ \hline \end{array}$	16. $\begin{array}{r} 83 \\ \times 7 \\ \hline \end{array}$	17. $\begin{array}{r} 38 \\ \times 4 \\ \hline \end{array}$	18. $\begin{array}{r} 65 \\ \times 4 \\ \hline \end{array}$
19. $\begin{array}{r} 82 \\ \times 9 \\ \hline \end{array}$	20. $\begin{array}{r} 53 \\ \times 7 \\ \hline \end{array}$	21. $\begin{array}{r} 97 \\ \times 2 \\ \hline \end{array}$	22. $\begin{array}{r} 49 \\ \times 4 \\ \hline \end{array}$	23. $\begin{array}{r} 29 \\ \times 8 \\ \hline \end{array}$	24. $\begin{array}{r} 76 \\ \times 5 \\ \hline \end{array}$
25. $\begin{array}{r} 93 \\ \times 5 \\ \hline \end{array}$	26. $\begin{array}{r} 74 \\ \times 6 \\ \hline \end{array}$	27. $\begin{array}{r} 85 \\ \times 7 \\ \hline \end{array}$	28. $\begin{array}{r} 59 \\ \times 3 \\ \hline \end{array}$	29. $\begin{array}{r} 62 \\ \times 6 \\ \hline \end{array}$	30. $\begin{array}{r} 47 \\ \times 4 \\ \hline \end{array}$
31. $\begin{array}{r} 231 \\ \times 2 \\ \hline \end{array}$	32. $\begin{array}{r} 122 \\ \times 3 \\ \hline \end{array}$	33. $\begin{array}{r} 322 \\ \times 2 \\ \hline \end{array}$	34. $\begin{array}{r} 210 \\ \times 4 \\ \hline \end{array}$	35. $\begin{array}{r} 412 \\ \times 2 \\ \hline \end{array}$	36. $\begin{array}{r} 120 \\ \times 3 \\ \hline \end{array}$
37. $\begin{array}{r} 118 \\ \times 3 \\ \hline \end{array}$	38. $\begin{array}{r} 218 \\ \times 2 \\ \hline \end{array}$	39. $\begin{array}{r} 229 \\ \times 4 \\ \hline \end{array}$	40. $\begin{array}{r} 407 \\ \times 2 \\ \hline \end{array}$	41. $\begin{array}{r} 235 \\ \times 3 \\ \hline \end{array}$	42. $\begin{array}{r} 346 \\ \times 2 \\ \hline \end{array}$
43. $\begin{array}{r} 184 \\ \times 2 \\ \hline \end{array}$	44. $\begin{array}{r} 492 \\ \times 2 \\ \hline \end{array}$	45. $\begin{array}{r} 292 \\ \times 4 \\ \hline \end{array}$	46. $\begin{array}{r} 353 \\ \times 2 \\ \hline \end{array}$	47. $\begin{array}{r} 381 \\ \times 4 \\ \hline \end{array}$	48. $\begin{array}{r} 462 \\ \times 3 \\ \hline \end{array}$

Helping at Home

Ask your child to write and solve multiplication problems based on the number of students in his or her class at school. How many ears do the students have altogether? How many toes? How many pencils if each has five pencils?

Multiplication

Multiply.

1.　37
　　× 2

2.　37
　　× 12

3.　64
　　× 4

4.　64
　　× 34

5.　24
　　× 3

6.　83
　　× 24

7.　24
　　× 13

8.　32
　　× 24

9.　24
　　× 11

10.　23
　　× 18

11.　52
　　× 34

12.　43
　　× 24

13.　34
　　× 12

14.　41
　　× 31

15.　23
　　× 15

16.　34
　　× 21

17.　53
　　× 13

18.　17
　　× 12

19.　42
　　× 31

20.　25
　　× 14

21.　32
　　× 25

22.　21
　　× 17

23.　35
　　× 11

24.　26
　　× 13

25.　30
　　× 29

26.　64
　　× 17

27.　84
　　× 50

28.　67
　　× 15

29.　53
　　× 41

30.　63
　　× 19

Helping at Home

Ask your child to solve one item on this page quickly as you keep time. Then, ask your child to solve the problem with a calculator as you keep time. Which strategy was faster? Talk about how knowing multiplication facts well increases speed.

Word Problems

Solve each problem.

1. The Cruisin' Coaster has 19 cars. If 37 people can ride in each car, how many people can ride at the same time?

2. The Jungle Adventure boats hold 14 people. If there are 24 boats, how many people can ride at the same time?

3. Harry and his friends waited 15 minutes in line for each ride. If they rode 38 rides, how many minutes did they spend waiting in line altogether?

4. Cory has 24 packages of sunflower seeds. If each package has 15 seeds, how many sunflower seeds does he have altogether?

5. Monica's yard measures 63' x 94'. How many square feet does she need to buy fertilizer for?

6. A ream of paper contains 500 sheets, and there are 10 reams in a case of paper. If Emily buys 30 cases, how many sheets of paper will she have?

7. An ant bed contains about 230 ants. If there are 6 of these beds on the playground, how many ants are there?

Helping at Home

Tell your child that the average person blinks about 15 times each minute. Ask your child to calculate how many times the average person blinks in five minutes. In twenty minutes? In one hour?

Division

Divide.

1. $4\overline{)76}$ 2. $3\overline{)91}$ 3. $5\overline{)86}$ 4. $6\overline{)50}$ 5. $2\overline{)35}$

6. $7\overline{)85}$ 7. $2\overline{)49}$ 8. $4\overline{)34}$ 9. $8\overline{)43}$ 10. $5\overline{)79}$

11. $4\overline{)312}$ 12. $8\overline{)674}$ 13. $3\overline{)497}$ 14. $4\overline{)406}$ 15. $2\overline{)677}$

16. $6\overline{)557}$ 17. $3\overline{)325}$ 18. $5\overline{)235}$ 19. $2\overline{)407}$ 20. $8\overline{)216}$

21. $3\overline{)276}$ 22. $8\overline{)728}$ 23. $4\overline{)108}$ 24. $7\overline{)441}$ 25. $5\overline{)336}$

Helping at Home

After your child completes this page, ask him or her to choose five items. Can your child write a related multiplication problem for each item?

Division

Divide.

1. $6\overline{)497}$ 2. $2\overline{)128}$ 3. $5\overline{)257}$ 4. $9\overline{)418}$

5. $6\overline{)678}$ 6. $5\overline{)2,516}$ 7. $3\overline{)8,437}$ 8. $3\overline{)2,076}$

9. $8\overline{)8,179}$ 10. $6\overline{)2,649}$ 11. $9\overline{)5,082}$ 12. $7\overline{)6,554}$

13. $5\overline{)9,479}$ 14. $2\overline{)4,236}$ 15. $3\overline{)6,879}$ 16. $2\overline{)6,671}$

17. $4\overline{)3,424}$ 18. $8\overline{)3,456}$ 19. $5\overline{)9,466}$ 20. $9\overline{)3,952}$

Helping at Home

Remind your child to align numbers carefully according to their place values when solving division problems. After your child completes several problems on this page, suggest that he or she use a colored pencil to draw vertical lines between the digits written to solve the problem.

Word Problems

Solve each problem.

1. Kyle is packaging jam in cartons. If each carton holds 9 bottles of jam, how many cartons will he need to package 1,934 bottles of jam?

2. Anna has 7,209 cans of soup that need to be boxed. If she puts 9 cans of soup in 1 box, how many boxes will she need?

3. Katherine has 9,315 sunflower seeds. She puts 7 seeds in each package. How many full packages of sunflower seeds does Katherine have when she is finished? How many seeds are left over?

4. Jermaine is bottling 6,488 ounces of root beer. One bottle holds 8 ounces. How many bottles will Jermaine have if he bottles all of the root beer?

5. Mario is packaging footballs in a box. Six footballs will fit in 1 box. How many boxes will Mario need if he has to package 288 footballs?

6. Katie has 2,837 flowers. If Katie puts 7 flowers in each vase, how many full vases will Katie have when she is finished?

7. Leo is bottling soda. Each bottle holds 7 ounces. How many bottles does Leo need if he has 2,786 ounces of soda to bottle?

8. Jenny is packaging fruit. She has 349 apples, 328 pears, and 548 oranges. If she puts 4 pieces of fruit in each package, how many full packages will she have when she is finished? How many pieces of fruit will be left?

Helping at Home Explain that the average person spends 1,638 hours each year involved in sports and leisure activities. Ask your child to calculate how many hours are spent in sports and leisure activities each month. Each week? Each day?

Equivalent Fractions

Fractions that equal the same amount are called **equivalent fractions**.

Example: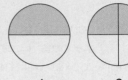

$$\frac{1}{2} = \frac{2}{4}$$

Write the equivalent fractions.

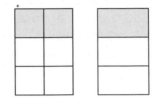

1. _____ = _____

2. _____ = _____

3. _____ = _____

4. _____ = _____

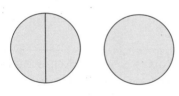

5. _____ = _____

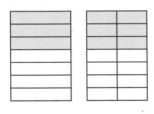

6. _____ = _____

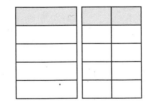

7. _____ = _____

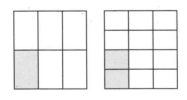

8. _____ = _____

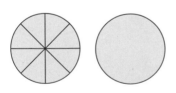

9. _____ = _____

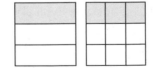

10. _____ = _____

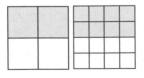

11. _____ = _____

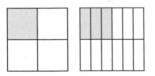

12. _____ = _____

Helping at Home

Ask your child to draw circles that represent pizzas. How many different ways can the pizzas be divided so that four people would each get an equal number of slices? Have your child write an equivalent fraction to show each person's serving for each pizza drawn.

Equivalent Fractions

Equivalent fractions are fractions that are equal. To find equivalent fractions, multiply any fraction by 1, or by another name for the number 1. Think about it as multiplying the numerator and the denominator by the same number.

$$\frac{1}{2} \times \frac{2}{2} = \frac{2}{4} \qquad \frac{1}{2} \times \frac{3}{3} = \frac{3}{6} \qquad \frac{1}{2} \times \frac{4}{4} = \frac{4}{8}$$

$\frac{1}{2}$ $\frac{2}{4}$

$\frac{3}{6}$ $\frac{4}{8}$

Cross out the fraction that is not equivalent to the first.

1. $\frac{1}{3}$ = $\frac{2}{6}$ $\frac{3}{9}$ $\frac{4}{8}$ $\frac{5}{15}$ $\frac{6}{18}$ 2. $\frac{1}{4}$ = $\frac{2}{8}$ $\frac{3}{6}$ $\frac{4}{16}$ $\frac{5}{20}$ $\frac{6}{24}$

3. $\frac{1}{5}$ = $\frac{2}{6}$ $\frac{2}{10}$ $\frac{3}{15}$ $\frac{4}{20}$ $\frac{5}{25}$ 4. $\frac{2}{3}$ = $\frac{4}{6}$ $\frac{6}{9}$ $\frac{8}{16}$ $\frac{10}{15}$ $\frac{12}{18}$

Fill in the missing number.

5. $\frac{1}{4}$ = $\frac{3}{\Box}$ 6. $\frac{2}{\Box}$ = $\frac{4}{6}$ 7. $\frac{5}{8}$ = $\frac{\Box}{16}$

8. $\frac{3}{4}$ = $\frac{9}{\Box}$ 9. $\frac{\Box}{6}$ = $\frac{2}{12}$ 10. $\frac{2}{3}$ = $\frac{\Box}{9}$

Helping at Home

After completing this page, ask your child to choose one item from items 5–10 to illustrate with partitioned circles. The illustration at the top of the page can serve as a model. Ask your child to tell how he or she knows that the fractions are equivalent.

Equivalent Fractions

Use equivalent fractions to rename one fraction or more in each pair. Then, add the fractions.

1. $\dfrac{4}{10}$ + $\dfrac{8}{100}$

2. $\dfrac{3}{100}$ + $\dfrac{7}{10}$

3. $\dfrac{1}{100}$ + $\dfrac{9}{10}$

4. $\dfrac{3}{10}$ + $\dfrac{7}{100}$

5. $\dfrac{9}{100}$ + $\dfrac{9}{10}$

6. $\dfrac{11}{10}$ + $\dfrac{11}{100}$

7. $\dfrac{2}{100}$ + $\dfrac{3}{10}$

8. $\dfrac{5}{10}$ + $\dfrac{7}{100}$

9. $\dfrac{2}{10}$ + $\dfrac{3}{100}$ + $\dfrac{1}{10}$

10. $\dfrac{5}{10}$ + $\dfrac{7}{100}$ + $\dfrac{5}{100}$

Helping at Home
Ask your child to explain how many zeros he or she added to the numerator and denominator of one fraction in each item on the page. Then, challenge your child to change both fractions in one item to equivalent fractions with a denominator of 1,000.

Comparing Fractions

To compare fractions, determine which figure has more area shaded. If necessary, calculate equivalent fractions and compare the numerators.

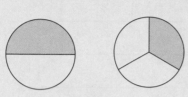

$$\frac{1}{2} = \frac{3}{6}$$

$$\frac{1}{3} = \frac{2}{6}$$

$$\frac{3}{6} \; \boxed{>} \; \frac{2}{6}$$

$$\frac{1}{2} \; \boxed{>} \; \frac{1}{3}$$

Write a fraction for the shaded area of each figure. Then, write <, >, or = to compare each pair of fractions.

1.

_____ ◯ _____

2.

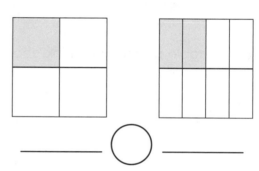

_____ ◯ _____

3.

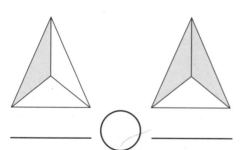

_____ ◯ _____

4.

_____ ◯ _____

5.

_____ ◯ _____

6.

_____ ◯ _____

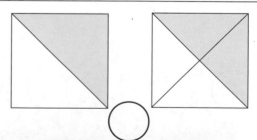

Helping at Home

After completing this page, ask your child to take the extra step of writing equivalent fractions with the same denominator for each pair of shapes. Which method of comparison does your child think is easier—comparing illustrations or comparing equivalent fractions?

Comparing Fractions

The more parts the whole is divided into, the smaller the fraction is.

$\frac{1}{2}$					
$\frac{1}{3}$					
$\frac{1}{4}$					
$\frac{1}{5}$					
$\frac{1}{6}$					
$\frac{1}{8}$					
$\frac{1}{10}$					
$\frac{1}{12}$					

Use the fraction table to help you think about which fraction is greater. Use >, <, or = to compare each pair of fractions.

1. $\frac{1}{2}$ ◯ $\frac{1}{4}$

2. $\frac{2}{3}$ ◯ $\frac{1}{3}$

3. $\frac{1}{4}$ ◯ $\frac{1}{6}$

4. $\frac{2}{6}$ ◯ $\frac{1}{3}$

5. $\frac{4}{8}$ ◯ $\frac{2}{10}$

6. $\frac{1}{12}$ ◯ $\frac{1}{10}$

7. $\frac{3}{4}$ ◯ $\frac{2}{8}$

8. $\frac{2}{5}$ ◯ $\frac{1}{3}$

9. $\frac{3}{8}$ ◯ $\frac{10}{12}$

10. $\frac{2}{8}$ ◯ $\frac{1}{4}$

11. $\frac{1}{5}$ ◯ $\frac{2}{10}$

12. $\frac{1}{3}$ ◯ $\frac{2}{4}$

13. $\frac{1}{6}$ ◯ $\frac{1}{3}$

14. $\frac{3}{12}$ ◯ $\frac{1}{3}$

15. $\frac{5}{10}$ ◯ $\frac{3}{6}$

16. $\frac{1}{2}$ ◯ $\frac{6}{10}$

Ask your child to use the chart at the top of this page to write a set of four equivalent fractions. For example, these fractions are equivalent: $\frac{1}{2}, \frac{3}{6}, \frac{4}{8}, \frac{6}{12}$.

Adding and Subtracting Fractions

To add or subtract fractions, the denominators must be the same. To add or subtract a fraction with a common denominator, follow these steps:

1. Check that the denominators are the same.

$$\frac{3}{8} + \frac{1}{8} =$$

$$\frac{3}{8} - \frac{1}{8} =$$

2. Add or subtract the numerators. Keep the same denominator.

$$\frac{3}{8} + \frac{1}{8} = \frac{4}{8}$$

$$\frac{3}{8} - \frac{1}{8} = \frac{2}{8}$$

3. Reduce to lowest terms.

$$\frac{4 \div 4}{8 \div 4} = \frac{1}{2}$$

$$\frac{2 \div 2}{8 \div 2} = \frac{1}{4}$$

Add or subtract.

1. $\dfrac{2}{4} + \dfrac{1}{4} =$

2. $\dfrac{6}{8} - \dfrac{4}{8} =$

3. $\dfrac{1}{5} + \dfrac{3}{5} =$

4. $\dfrac{4}{10} + \dfrac{5}{10} =$

5. $\dfrac{7}{8} - \dfrac{5}{8} =$

6. $\dfrac{9}{10} - \dfrac{3}{10} =$

7. $\dfrac{6}{9} + \dfrac{2}{9} =$

8. $\dfrac{10}{12} - \dfrac{6}{12} =$

9. $\dfrac{15}{20} - \dfrac{7}{20} =$

10. $\dfrac{68}{100} + \dfrac{12}{100} =$

11. $\dfrac{5}{50} + \dfrac{15}{50} =$

12. $\dfrac{12}{15} - \dfrac{9}{15} =$

Helping at Home

Explain that the answer to a fractions problem should always be simplified, or reduced to its lowest terms. To help your child with this step, ask him or her to name three fractions that can be simplified to $\frac{1}{2}$ and three that can be simplified to $\frac{1}{4}$.

Adding and Subtracting Fractions

To add or subtract fractions when the denominators are the same, you just add or subtract the numerators. The denominators do not change. Try to picture each problem in your head.

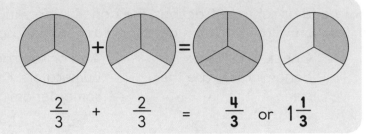

$$\frac{2}{3} + \frac{2}{3} = \frac{4}{3} \text{ or } 1\frac{1}{3}$$

Add or subtract.

1. $\frac{2}{6}$
   $-\ \frac{1}{6}$

2. $\frac{3}{4}$
   $+\ \frac{1}{4}$

3. $\frac{6}{8}$
   $-\ \frac{5}{8}$

4. $\frac{10}{12}$
   $+\ \frac{14}{12}$

5. $\frac{4}{5}$
   $+\ \frac{1}{5}$

6. $\frac{7}{8}$
   $+\ \frac{4}{8}$

7. $\frac{9}{11}$
   $+\ \frac{2}{11}$

8. $\frac{4}{7}$
   $+\ \frac{5}{7}$

9. $\frac{3}{10}$
   $+\ \frac{3}{10}$

10. $\frac{4}{9}$
   $+\ \frac{6}{9}$

11. $\frac{8}{12}$
   $-\ \frac{2}{12}$

12. $\frac{5}{13}$
   $+\ \frac{12}{13}$

Helping at Home
After completing this page, ask your child to use the visual aid at the top of the page as a model for drawing an illustration for another item. How many shapes are solid, or all filled in, in your child's drawing? What number do they represent? (Answer: 1)

Word Problems

The students in Mr. King's gym class are completing a 1-mile obstacle course in groups of 4. Each student on the team will complete a part of the course, but they do not have to complete equal parts. Kate, Sarah, Ethan, and James form one of the four-person teams. Read each problem and solve using the information in the table below.

$\frac{1}{8}$ mile	$\frac{2}{8}$ mile	$\frac{1}{8}$ mile	$\frac{1}{8}$ mile	$\frac{3}{8}$ mile
Backwards Run	Skip	Run Through Tires	Crab Walk	Sprint

1. Kate loves to skip, so she has asked her team for that part of the race. How many miles are left for her teammates?

2. Ethan wants to do the crab walk and the sprint, but Sarah says that is not fair. Why do you think that Sarah thinks it is unfair?

3. If Kate skips, Sarah runs backwards, and James runs through tires and completes the crab walk, how many miles, and what events, are left for Ethan?

4. Is it possible for a four-person team to give each person an equal part of the race? Why or why not?

5. In order for each child to complete the same amount, how many miles should each complete? Write an addition equation that supports your answer.

Helping at Home
Ask your child to use the visual aid at the top of this page to write another word problem based on the information. Can you solve the problem your child wrote? Write a problem for your child to solve, too.

Mixed Numbers

This fraction shows $\frac{5}{3}$. Five-thirds is called an **improper fraction** because the numerator is larger than the denominator. Three-thirds $\left(\frac{3}{3}\right)$ equals 1 whole, so $\frac{5}{3}$ equals 1 whole and $\frac{2}{3}$. One and two-thirds $\left(1\frac{2}{3}\right)$ is called a **mixed number**.

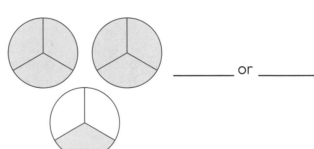

$\frac{5}{3}$ or $1\frac{2}{3}$

Write each fraction as an improper fraction and as a mixed number.

1.

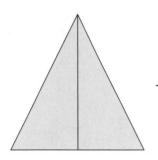

_____ or _____

2.

_____ or _____

3.

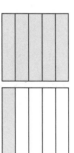

_____ or _____

4.

_____ or _____

5.

_____ or _____

6.

_____ or _____

Adding Mixed Numbers

1. Find the least common denominator and equivalent fractions if necessary.

$3\frac{2}{3}$ $\frac{2 \times 3}{3 \times 3} = \frac{6}{9}$

$+ 2\frac{7}{9}$ $\frac{7 \times 1}{9 \times 1} = \frac{7}{9}$

2. Add.

$3\frac{6}{9}$

$+ 2\frac{7}{9}$

$5\frac{13}{9}$

3. Reduce and regroup if necessary.

$3\frac{6}{9}$

$+ 2\frac{7}{9}$

$5\frac{13}{9} = 6\frac{4}{9}$

Add.

1. $1\frac{1}{5}$
    $+ 3\frac{3}{5}$

2. $2\frac{4}{10}$
    $+ 7\frac{4}{10}$

3. $5\frac{4}{14}$
    $+ 4\frac{5}{14}$

4. $3\frac{3}{10}$
    $+ 3\frac{2}{10}$

5. $4\frac{8}{12}$
    $+ 6\frac{9}{12}$

6. $1\frac{6}{8}$
    $+ 1\frac{5}{8}$

7. $3\frac{6}{9}$
    $+ 5\frac{5}{9}$

8. $6\frac{6}{12}$
    $+ \ \frac{8}{12}$

9. $6\frac{5}{10}$
    $+ 6\frac{9}{10}$

10. $1\frac{4}{6}$
    $+ 2\frac{5}{6}$

11. $3\frac{9}{15}$
    $+ 4\frac{8}{15}$

12. $3\frac{8}{12}$
    $+ 2\frac{5}{12}$

Helping at Home
Ask your child to name three items he or she would like to receive as birthday gifts. Have your child research the price of each, round it to the nearest ten cents, and write it as a mixed number (example: $12.68 = 12\frac{7}{10}$). What is the sum of the prices?

Subtracting Mixed Numbers

Rewrite $3\frac{1}{4}$ so that you can subtract.

$$3\frac{1}{4} = 2 + 1\frac{1}{4} = 2\frac{5}{4}$$

$$-1\frac{3}{4} \longrightarrow 1\frac{3}{4}$$

$$1\frac{2}{4} = 1\frac{1}{2}$$

Rewrite $6\frac{2}{9}$ so that you can subtract.

$$6\frac{2}{9} = 5 + 1\frac{2}{9} = 5\frac{11}{9}$$

$$-5\frac{4}{9} \longrightarrow 5\frac{4}{9}$$

$$\frac{7}{9}$$

Subtract.

1. $3\frac{3}{7}$
$-1\frac{5}{7}$

2. $5\frac{1}{3}$
$-2\frac{2}{3}$

3. $4\frac{1}{6}$
$-3\frac{5}{6}$

4. $8\frac{3}{8}$
$-2\frac{5}{8}$

5. $6\frac{1}{5}$
$-3\frac{3}{5}$

6. $4\frac{3}{10}$
$-3\frac{7}{10}$

7. $8\frac{2}{5}$
$-5\frac{4}{5}$

8. $10\frac{5}{12}$
$-7\frac{7}{12}$

9. $3\frac{1}{8}$
$-2\frac{5}{8}$

10. $6\frac{4}{9}$
$-5\frac{7}{9}$

11. $12\frac{5}{12}$
$-10\frac{7}{12}$

12. $9\frac{1}{4}$
$-3\frac{3}{4}$

Helping at Home
Demonstrate another way to solve problems on this page. Change each mixed number to a fraction. Subtract the second numerator from the first. Change the answer back to a mixed number.
For item #1: $\frac{24}{7} - \frac{12}{7} = \frac{12}{7}$ or $1\frac{5}{7}$.

Multiplying Whole Numbers and Fractions

$8 \times \dfrac{3}{8} = \dfrac{8}{1} \times \dfrac{3}{8}$

$= \dfrac{8 \times 3}{1 \times 8}$

$= \dfrac{24}{8}$

$= 3$

1. Rewrite the whole number as a fraction. (Write a denominator of 1.)
2. Multiply the numerators.
3. Multiply the denominators.
4. Simplify if possible.

$\dfrac{3}{4} \times 6 = \dfrac{3}{4} \times \dfrac{6}{1}$

$= \dfrac{3 \times 6}{4 \times 1}$

$= \dfrac{18}{4}$

$= 4\dfrac{2}{4} = 4\dfrac{1}{2}$

Solve each problem.

1. $3 \times \dfrac{2}{3} =$

2. $\dfrac{4}{5} \times 2 =$

3. $1 \times \dfrac{6}{7} =$

4. $2 \times \dfrac{4}{7} =$

5. $\dfrac{2}{5} \times 6 =$

6. $3 \times \dfrac{3}{10} =$

7. $9 \times \dfrac{3}{4} =$

8. $6 \times \dfrac{3}{10} =$

9. $8 \times \dfrac{1}{6} =$

10. $2 \times \dfrac{6}{7} =$

11. $6 \times \dfrac{1}{10} =$

12. $\dfrac{3}{8} \times 4 =$

13. $\dfrac{3}{10} \times 5 =$

14. $5 \times \dfrac{2}{9} =$

15. $\dfrac{3}{7} \times 2 =$

16. $\dfrac{2}{3} \times 4 =$

Helping at Home Help your child better understand the problems on this page by asking him or her to change each to a whole number multiplied by a fraction with a numerator of 1. For example, change item #1 to $6 \times \dfrac{1}{3}$ and item #2 to $\dfrac{1}{5} \times 8$.

Word Problems

1. Jacob's class has 24 students. If $\frac{1}{8}$ of them play the piano, how many students in his class play the piano?

2. There are 12 students working in the library. If $\frac{3}{4}$ of them are girls, how many girls are working in the library?

3. Six students are working on math. Two-thirds of them are working on fractions. How many students are working on fractions?

4. There are 20 students at lunch. One-fifth of the students are in the hall. How many students are in the hall?

5. Last night, 18 students read before bed. One-third of them read a comic book. How many students read a comic book?

6. In a class of 24 students, $\frac{7}{8}$ are allowed to attend recess on Friday. How many students will attend recess?

Helping at Home

Ask your child to write word problems based on the number of students in his or her class. For example, if $\frac{1}{3}$ of the students ride the bus, how many ride the bus? Can you solve the problems your child writes? Write problems for your child, too.

Decimals: Tenths

A **tenth** is the first digit after the decimal point. It is one part of 10. To find a tenth, count the number of boxes out of 10 that are shaded.

Example: Find the number of tenths in the box.

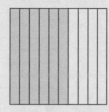

Six-tenths of the box is shaded.

When there are no whole numbers, place a 0 before the decimal point.

The total can be written as 0.6, $\frac{6}{10}$, or $\frac{3}{5}$.

Find the number of tenths in each box. Write the total as a fraction and as a decimal.

1.

Fraction: _____

Decimal: _____

2.

Fraction: _____

Decimal: _____

3.

Fraction: _____

Decimal: _____

4.
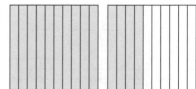

Fraction: _____

Decimal: _____

5.

Fraction: _____

Decimal: _____

6.

Fraction: _____

Decimal: _____

Helping at Home

Explain to your child that if you had 6 dimes, you would have $\frac{6}{10}$ of one dollar, or .60¢. Ask your child to write a fraction and decimal to show 3 dimes, 7 dimes, and 9 dimes. Have your child manipulate real dimes if it helps him or her.

Decimals: Hundredths

A **hundredth** is the second digit after the decimal point. It is one part of 100. To find a hundredth, count the number of boxes out of 100 that are shaded.

Example: Find the number of hundredths in the box.

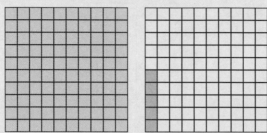

One whole box is shaded and five hundredths of the second box is shaded.

The total can be written as 1.05, $1\frac{5}{100}$, or $1\frac{1}{20}$.

Find the number of hundredths in each box. Write the total as a fraction in lowest terms and as a decimal.

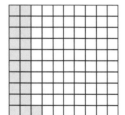

1. Fraction: _____

   Decimal: _____

2. Fraction: _____

   Decimal: _____

3. Fraction: _____

   Decimal: _____

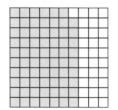

4. Fraction: _____

   Decimal: _____

5. Fraction: _____

   Decimal: _____

6. Fraction: _____

   Decimal: _____

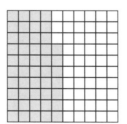

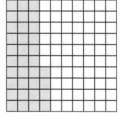

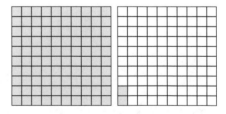

Helping at Home

Explain to your child that if you had 2 pennies, you would have $\frac{2}{100}$ of one dollar, or .02¢. Ask your child to write a fraction and decimal to show 4 pennies, 7 pennies, and 14 pennies. Have your child manipulate real pennies if it helps him or her.

Decimal Notation

To write decimals in word form, write the word *and* as the decimal point.

Example: twenty-six and forty-two hundredths = 26.42 = $26\frac{42}{100}$ = $26\frac{21}{50}$

Write the decimal equivalent.

1. nine and sixteen-hundredths _____

2. fourteen and seventy-two hundredths _____

3. two hundred and thirty-four hundredths _____

4. forty-seven and eighty-nine hundredths _____

5. eleven and sixty-two hundredths _____

Write the equivalent fraction or mixed number for each decimal in lowest terms.

6.	0.08 _____		7.	6.09 _____		8.	2.12 _____	
9.	0.21 _____		10.	7.34 _____		11.	0.55 _____	
12.	16.08 _____		13.	300.24 _____		14.	25.04 _____	
15.	600.49 _____		16.	0.72 _____		17.	0.22 _____	
18.	25.34 _____		19.	9.09 _____		20.	4.39 _____	

Helping at Home

Have your child go to www.olympic.org and find records for the men's or women's 100-meter dash. Ask your child to read several times aloud, using *and* in place of the decimal point.

Ordering Decimals

To order decimals with whole numbers, treat the whole numbers like decimals. For example, whole numbers would be written as 1.0, 2.0, and 3.0. Then, order the numbers. On the number lines below, each mark represents one-tenth.

Write the missing decimals.

1.

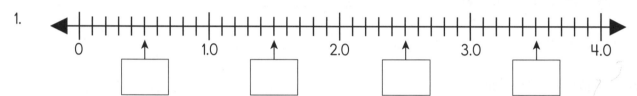

2.

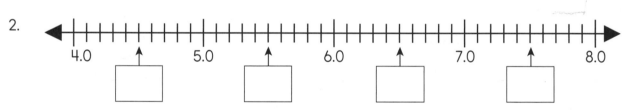

Write the numbers in order from least to greatest.

3.
2	0.5	1	1.5

4.
2.5	1.5	2	3

5.
3	3.5	2.5	0.5

6.
3.5	2.5	5.5	4.5	4

Comparing Decimals

To compare decimals, follow these steps:

1. Look at the number of digits to the left of the decimal point. The number with the most digits is greatest.
2. If the number of digits is the same, begin with the first digit on the left. The larger digit is the greater number.
3. If the digits are the same, move to the next place value and find the larger digit.
4. Continue from left to right until you find a digit in the same place value with a greater value.

Example: 0.4 (>) 0.2   0.13 (<) 0.34

Write > or < to compare each pair of decimals.

1.   0.6 ◯ 0.4

2.   0.1 ◯ 0.5

3.   0.23 ◯ 0.03

4.   0.6 ◯ 0.9

5.   0.06 ◯ 0.60

6.   0.4 ◯ 0.7

7.   0.9 ◯ 0.5

8.   0.7 ◯ 0.6

9.   0.42 ◯ 0.14

10.   0.72 ◯ 0.27

11.   0.25 ◯ 0.52

12.   0.7 ◯ 0.3

13.   1.4 ◯ 1.6

14.   3.5 ◯ 3.7

15.   16.2 ◯ 16.8

Helping at Home
For several items on this page, ask your child to write each decimal number as a fraction and compare again. Is the answer the same? Why?

Converting Measurements

1 gram (g) = 1,000 milligrams (mg)

1,000 grams (g) = 1 kilogram (kg)

Find the missing numbers.

1. 3 g = _____ mg

2. 8,000 mg = _____ g

3. 14,000 g = _____ kg

4. 84,000 g = _____ kg

5. 9 g = _____ mg

6. 41,000 g = _____ kg

7. 73 g = _____ mg

8. 57,000 mg = _____ g

9. 25,000 g = _____ kg

10. 7,000 g = _____ kg

11. 12 g = _____ mg

12. 118,000 g = _____ kg

13. 6,000 g = _____ kg

14. 2,000 mg = _____ g

15. 65 g = _____ mg

Answer each question.

16. Megan uses 4,000 milligrams of sugar in her recipe. How many grams of sugar does she use?

17. Harry measures 15 grams of salt. How many milligrams does he measure?

18. Jake's book weighs 2 kilograms. How many grams does his book weigh?

19. Peter's recipe calls for 16,000 milligrams of cocoa. How many grams of cocoa does Peter need?

Sixteen ounces equal one pound. Ask your child to calculate his or her weight in ounces. Can he or she find a product in the kitchen with a weight given in ounces and convert it to a fraction of a pound?

Helping at Home

Converting Measurements

1 liter (L) = 1,000 milliliters (mL)

Find the missing numbers.

1. 8 L = _____ mL

2. 5,000 mL = _____ L

3. 15 L = _____ mL

4. 48,000 mL = _____ L

5. 4 L = _____ mL

6. 33,000 mL = _____ L

7. 92 L = _____ mL

8. 21 L = _____ mL

9. 7,000 mL = _____ L

10. 6 L = _____ mL

11. 8,000 mL = _____ L

12. 27 L = _____ mL

Answer each question.

13. William measures 18,000 milliliters of milk. How many liters does he measure?

14. Kim drinks $\frac{1}{2}$ of a liter of soda. How many milliliters does she drink?

15. Mark pours 14 liters of juice at the party. How many milliliters of juice does he pour?

16. Isabelle buys 15 2-liter bottles of soda for the party. Her guests drink 18,000 milliliters. How many liters of soda does Isabelle have left over? How many 2-liter bottles does she have left over?

Word Problems: Time

Solve each problem.

1. What time will it be in 2 hours and 15 minutes?

2. What time was it 5 hours and 30 minutes ago?

3. What time was it 3 hours ago?

4. What time will it be in 3 hours and 45 minutes?

5. What time was it 4 hours and 15 minutes ago?

6. What time will it be in 1 hour and 30 minutes?

7. What time was it 2 hours and 30 minutes ago?

8. What time will it be in 6 hours and 15 minutes?

9. Rudy left 25 minutes before his soccer lesson began. If his soccer lesson started at 2:45 pm, what time did Rudy leave?

10. Terrance has 50 minutes left to shop before the mall closes. It is 9:05 pm. What time does the mall close?

11. Amber arrived 15 minutes early for her dentist appointment. If her appointment was scheduled for 7:45 am, what time did Amber arrive at the dentist's office?

12. Carla left the movie at 9:15 pm. She stopped for 30 minutes to eat dinner. Then, it took her 15 minutes to drive home. What time did Carla get home?

Helping at Home

Ask your child to write word problems about how he or she spends time in a typical day. How much time passes between leaving for school and returning to school? How many hours does he or she usually sleep each night?

Word Problems: Money

Kyle and his friends are shopping for their party. Use the shopping list below to solve each problem.

Shopping List	
paper plates	$1.49
cups	$2.59
soda (2-liter bottle)	$1.19
napkins	$1.15
cake	$15.45
ice cream	$2.69
candy	$4.75
party favors	$9.25

1. Kyle buys 3 packages of paper plates and 4 packages of cups. How much does he spend altogether?

2. Leslie buys 3 packages of candy. She pays with a $20 bill. How much change does she get back?

3. Kathryn buys 13 2-liter bottles of soda for the party. She only has a $10 bill. How much more money does she need?

4. Nicole buys 5 packages of party favors and 3 packages of candy. How much more does she spend on party favors than candy?

5. Amy sends 135 party invitations. If she spends 15¢ to mail each invitation, how much money does she spend on postage altogether?

6. Pete buys a cake and 2 cartons of ice cream. He has 2 ten-dollar bills, 1 five-dollar bill, and 2 quarters in his wallet. How much will he have left in his wallet after he buys the items for the party?

Helping at Home

Ask your child to imagine receiving $500 to spend in any way he or she likes. How many items would he or she buy? What is the approximate price of each item? How much money would be left after purchasing each item?

Perimeter

Remember, to find the **perimeter** of a figure, add the lengths of all the sides of the figure.

Find the perimeter.

1.

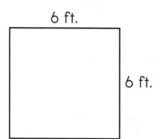

2.

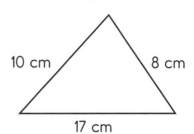

3.

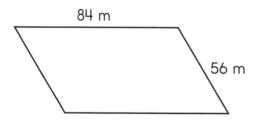

4.

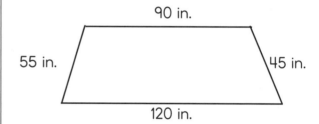

Solve each problem.

5. Jeff is making a rectangular picture frame. If the frame is 36" × 24", what is the perimeter of the frame?

6. Lisa needs enough trim to go around the edge of her quilt. If the quilt measures 96" × 72", how many inches of trim will Lisa beed to buy?

7. Greg is building a dog pen. Two of the sides are 45', and the other two sides are 28'. How many feet of fencing will Greg need?

8. Reid is gluing string around the edge of his kite. If the sides measure 12", 16", 14", and 13", how many inches of string does Reid need?

Helping at Home

Ask your child to measure each wall of a room in your home and find the room's perimeter in feet, yards, and inches. Is it necessary for your child to measure all four walls? Why or why not?

Area

Remember, to find the **area** of a rectangular figure, multiply the length by the width.

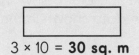

3 × 10 = **30 sq. m**

Find the area of each shape.

1.
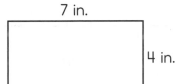
7 in.

4 in.

2.
8 m

8 m

3.
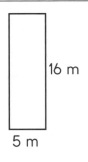
16 m

5 m

4.
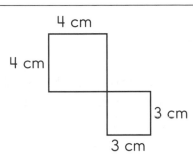
4 cm

4 cm

3 cm

3 cm

Solve each problem.

5. Holly makes a rectangular kite that is 15" × 28". What is the area of Holly's kite?

6. Linden frames a poster that is 25" × 39". What is the area of Linden's poster?

7. If Maria's garden measures 6 yd. × 9 yd, what is the area of her garden?

8. Travis buys a piece of canvas for his project that measures 15' × 33'. What is the area of the canvas?

Helping at Home Ask your child to find the area of one room of your home in square feet. Then, have your child research the cost of carpet or other flooring per square foot. How much would it cost to have new flooring installed in the room?

Line Plots

The line plot below shows the lengths of some common bugs found in and around houses. Use the data shown in the line plot to answer the questions.

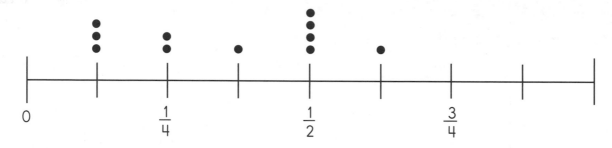

1. What is the difference in length in inches between the longest and shortest bugs?

2. The term *mode* stands for the number that appears most in a data set. Which bug length would be the mode for this data set?

3. Measure the bug below and place an additional X on the line plot for this bug.

4. With the additional data you just entered on the line plot, what is the difference between the longest and shortest bugs?

© Carson-Dellosa • CD-704504

Understanding Angles

The point at which two rays meet to form an angle is called a **vertex**. Point N is the vertex.

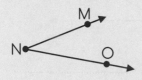

An angle that is less than 90° is called an **acute** angle.

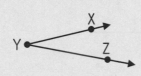

An angle that is 90° is called a **right** angle.

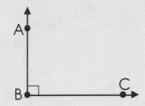

An angle that is greater than 90° is called an **obtuse** angle.

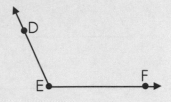

Identify each angle below as either acute, right, or obtuse.

1.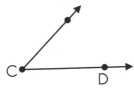

_____

2.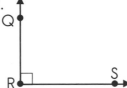

_____

3.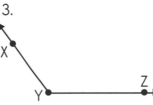

_____

4.

_____

5.

_____

6.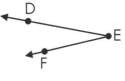

_____

7.

_____

8.

_____

Helping at Home

While traveling in the car, ask your child to look for real-world examples of acute, right, and obtuse angles. For example, a tree trunk and limb might form an acute angle and the corner of a sign might form a right angle.

Measuring Angles

Use a protractor to measure each angle. Then, identify each angle as acute, right, or obtuse.

1.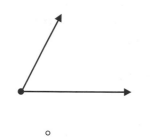

_____°, _____

2.

_____°, _____

3.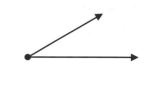

_____°, _____

4.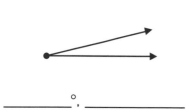

_____°, _____

5.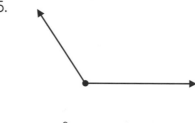

_____°, _____

6.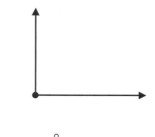

_____°, _____

7.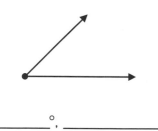

_____°, _____

8.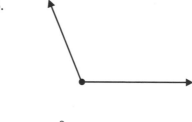

_____°, _____

9.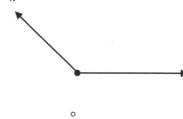

_____°, _____

Draw an angle with the given measurement.

10. 30 degrees

11. 110 degrees

12. 80 degrees

Helping at Home

Have your child use a compass or tracing to draw a large circle on blank paper. Show how to use a straightedge to divide the circle into 360 equal parts. Explain that each part represents a one-degree angle that can be used to measure angles.

Adding Angle Measurements

Calculate the measurement of x.

1.

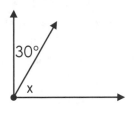

x = _____ °

2.

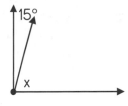

x = _____ °

3.

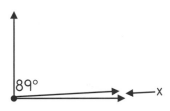

x = _____ °

4.

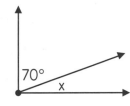

x = _____ °

5.

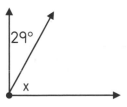

x = _____ °

6.

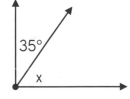

x = _____ °

7.

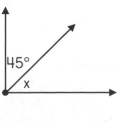

x = _____ °

8.

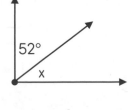

x = _____ °

Helping at Home Hold one arm straight up and one arm straight out to form a 90° angle. Then, name angle measurements such as 20° and 45°. Can your child point to the approximate spot between your arms where the line would be to form that angle?

Types of Lines

A **line segment** is a finite portion of a line that contains two endpoints. This figure is named $\overline{XY}$.

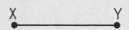

A **line** is a set of points in a straight path that extends infinitely in two directions. This figure is named $\overleftrightarrow{CD}$.

A **ray** is a portion of a line that extends from one endpoint infinitely in one direction. This figure is named $\overrightarrow{TX}$.

Lines that never cross are called **parallel lines**.

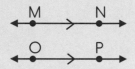

Lines that cross are called **intersecting lines**.

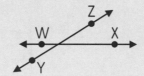

Lines that cross at right angles are called **perpendicular lines**.

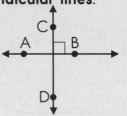

Name each line segment, line, or ray.

1.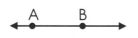

_____

2.

_____

3.

_____

4.

_____

5.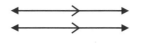

_____

6.

_____

Identify each figure as parallel lines, intersecting lines, or perpendicular lines.

7.

_____

8.

_____

9.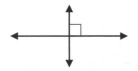

_____

© Carson-Dellosa • CD-704504

Parallel and Perpendicular Lines

Parallel lines are lines that never intersect.
Perpendicular lines are lines that form right angles where they intersect.

Draw a line parallel to each line segment below.

1.

2.

3.

4.

5.

6.

Draw a line perpendicular to each line segment below.

7.

8.

9.

10.

11.

12.

Helping at Home

Ask your child to look at a printed or online street map of your neighborhood or town. Can he or she find examples of perpendicular and parallel lines?

Triangles

A **scalene** triangle has 0 sides that are equal in length.
An **isosceles** triangle has 2 sides that are equal in length.
An **equilateral** triangle has 3 sides that are equal in length.

Identify each triangle as scalene, isosceles, or equilateral.

1.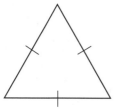

_____

2.

_____

3.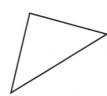

_____

4.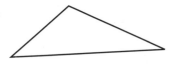

_____

5.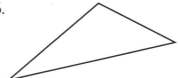

_____

6.

_____

An **acute** angle is less than 90 degrees.
A **right** angle equals 90 degrees.
An **obtuse** angle is greater than 90 degrees.

Identify each angle as acute, right, or obtuse.

7.

_____

8.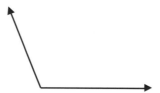

_____

9.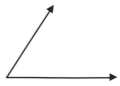

_____

10.

_____

11.

_____

12.

_____

Helping at Home Explain that a right triangle, as shown in item #2 on this page, contains a right angle made from perpendicular lines. Ask your child to look for real-world examples of right triangles. What other shapes contain right angles?

Symmetry

A **line of symmetry** is a line that divides a figure into two identical parts. If a figure has one or more lines of symmetry, the figure is **symmetrical**. Some figures have many lines of symmetry. These figures are symmetrical.

Identify whether each figure is symmetrical by writing *yes* or *no*.

1.

2.

3.

4.

5.

_____

6.

7.

8.

9.

10.

_____

11.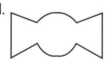

12.

13.

14.

15.

_____

Draw all of the lines of symmetry on each figure.

16.

17.

18.

19.

20.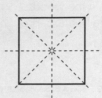

Helping at Home

Ask your child to think about symmetry found in people and animals. Most creatures have two identical or nearly identical sides. Are there any animals whose bodies are not symmetrical? Have your child do some research to find out.

Answer Key

Page 10
1. to be in a warm climate; 2. going camping; 3. often had afternoon showers; 4. for a long weekend; 5. in the woods; 6. in a lake; 7. not too far from home; 8. brought back fish

Page 11
1. A; 2. B; 3. C; 4–6. Answers will vary.

Page 13
1–5. Answers will vary. 6. The Inuit live in the Arctic regions of the US, Canada, Greenland, and Siberia.

Page 14
1. Friendly; 2. eleven; 3. sweet; 4. rabbit; 5. beagle; 6. Travers; 7. Becky; 8. mean; 9. Preston; 10. Sunday; 11. Marty; 12. Shiloh; The book received the Newbery Medal.

Page 15
1. Answers will vary but should include that the dogs were strays, that their new owners eventually loved them. 2. Marty found his dog by the river; Old Yeller showed up on Travis's farm. 3. Answers will vary.

Page 16
1. She prefers to be alone. 2. Answers will vary. 3. Answers will vary but may include observant, kind, thoughtful, heroic.

Page 17
1. Astronomy; 2. especially; 3. planetarium; 4. telescope; 5. conditions; 6. observations; 7. constellations; 8. over; 9. compass; 10. expedition

Page 19
1–6. Answers will vary. 7. mid and night, street and car; 8. bare and foot; 9. a kind of fruit; 10. a period of not eating food; 11. to grow old; 12. put up with

Page 20
1.–2. first person, author; 3.–4. third person, Tony and Jose; 5.–6. third person, Erin

Page 21
1. Ancient civilizations did not have scientific information that explained the causes of earthquakes. 2. Some Native Americans thought a giant sea turtle held up Earth. 3. In India, it was believed that four elephants held up Earth. 4. The ancient Greeks thought earthquakes showed the gods' anger.

Page 23
1. B; 2. A; 3. Calcium helps strengthen teeth. 4. Fluoride reduces the number of cavities. 5. The Importance of Dental Floss: removes accumulated plaque; William Addis: invented the toothbrush, used bone and hairbrush bristles; Tooth Cleaners Over the Years: scratched their teeth with sticks, wiped their teeth with rags, chewed on crushed bones or shells; Tooth Cleaning Today: fluoride toothpaste, dental floss, specially angled toothbrushes

Page 25
1. No one had studied the sky with a telescope until Galileo in the sixteenth century. 2. jeudi; 3. the sun, the moon, Mars, Mercury, Jupiter, Venus, and Saturn; 4. Saturn; 5. Friday's child is loving and giving. 6. C; 7. E; 8. A; 9. D; 10. B; 11. The year was broken into weeks. 12. Some days were named after Nordic and Anglo-Saxon gods.

© Carson-Dellosa • CD-704504

Answer Key

Page 26

Gastropods	Bivalves	Chitons
single, coiled shells	two shells hinged together at one end or along one side	8 shell plates that look like a turtle's shell
beaches of the Atlantic and Pacific Oceans in North America	coasts of the Atlantic and Pacific Oceans in North America	shallow rock pools in Pacific Ocean from Alaska to Mexico
limpets, snails, slugs, whelks	clams, mussels, oysters, scallops	Merten's chiton, northern red chiton, mossy mopalia

Page 27
1. range; 2. incorporated; 3. natives;
4. contingent; 5. stalked; 6. accuracy;
7. weirs; 8. culture

Page 28
1. Asia; 2. Nile, Amazon; 3. Australia, Europe;
4. Australia; 5. Mount Everest, Mount McKinley, Aconcagua

Page 29
1. four; 2. Cenozoic, Mesozoic, Paleozoic, Precambrian; 3. Mesozoic; 4. three;
5. Cretaceous, Jurassic, Triassic; 6. Cenozoic

Page 31
1. The silky brown bat is attracted to it.
2. nocturnal animals; 3. They don't need any color because they attract by smell, not sight. 4. its proboscis; 5. If the pollen was wet, it would be in a clump and wouldn't stick. 6. 1. What a way to spend a day! 2. There are some you just don't want to get near. 7. I; 8. D; 9. G; 10. F; 11. H; 12. B; 13. J; 14. A; 15. E; 16; C; 17. open again; 18. not noticeable

Page 33
1–8. Answers will vary. Paragraph should match interview notes.

Page 34
1. J; 2. C 3. M; 4. L; 5. O; 6. F; 7. A; 8. N; 9. G; 10. B; 11. I; 12. K; 13. H; 14. E; 15. D

Page 35
Answers will vary.

Page 36
Answers will vary.

Page 37
Answers will vary.

Page 38
Examples and details will vary.

Page 39
1. Accept any appropriate topic. Notes should include significant facts and details. 2. The list should include three or more words and definitions that pertain to the topic. 3. Observe use of some of the suggested linking words. 4. Essays will vary. 5. Illustrations will vary.

Page 41
Paragraphs will vary but should be five sentences long and include the topic sentence and surrounding details from the graphic organizer.

Page 42
Essays will vary but must include at least six time-order words.

Page 43
Story beginnings will vary but should include some words from the Onomatopoeia and Five Senses Word Banks.

Page 44
1–3. Answers will vary.

Answer Key

Page 45
Paragraphs will vary but should include a satisfying ending.

Page 46
Stories will vary but should include dialogue.

Page 48
1. that; 2. whom; 3. whomever; 4. Whichever; 5. Whoever; 6. whose; 7. which; 8. who; 9. where; 10. when; 11. why; 12. when

Page 49
1. was writing, am writing, will be writing; 2. was swimming; am swimming; will be swimming; 3. was reading; am reading; will be reading; 4. was playing; am playing; will be playing; 5. was eating; am eating; will be eating; 6. was sitting; am sitting; will be sitting; 7. am playing; 8. will be playing; 9. was playing; 10. could; 11. might; 12. must; 13. shall; 14. would

Page 50
1–5. Answers will vary but must be complete sentences with complete subjects and predicates. 6. (boxed) The gentle manatee (circled) lives in shallow water.
7. (underlined) sometimes called sea cows; Answers will vary. 8. (boxed) Most West Indian manatees (circled) live in Florida. 9. (boxed) They (circled) look for food at the water's surface. 10. (underlined) A resting manatee; Answers will vary. 11. (boxed) The average adult manatee (circled) is three meters (9.8 feet) long. 12. (boxed) Manatees (circled) eat all types of plants.

Page 51
1. big, black; 2. delicious, chocolate; 3. six, empty; 4. long, green; 5. pretty, new; 6. between the cracks; 7. for my lunch; 8. on the steps; 9. from a nearby college; 10. about my behavior; 11. It's, its; 12. by, buy; 13. hare, hair; 14. to, too, two; 15. there, their, they're

Page 52
1. "Can we please stay for 10 more minutes?" the children asked. 2. "I knew about the surprise party all along," Jonah admitted. 3. "That was a really silly joke," Alyssa giggled. 4. "I think I have a cold, so don't get too close," Maggie warned.
5. "Shh, she might hear us," Liz whispered. 6. "I didn't mean to do it, but I couldn't help myself," Serena confessed. 7. "You can do it," the coach cheered. 8. "First, line up all the numbers, and then add them," the teacher explained. 9. "The water in the pool is chilly today," the lifeguard warned. 10. "Stir the ingredients well," the cooking instructor suggested.

Page 53
1. "I thought about taking a bus, but I finally decided to take an airplane," Emily said. 2. "I am not sure," Tony sighed. "I just can't remember where I left my keys." 3. "The treasure is hidden in the forest," the prince whispered. 4. "Did you see where Melinda went?" Tyler asked. "I want to invite her over for lunch." 5. Sue asked, "Do you know how to grow an herb garden?" 6. "I want to learn to play the cello," Maria said. "Will you teach me?" 7. "Jelly beans are my favorite!" Daniel shouted. "I love the cherry-flavored ones."

Page 54
world, nights, Krusades, liturature, catolog, yung, write, sektion, for, beutiful, desined, staned. 1. world; 2. knights; 3. Crusades; 4. literature; 5 catalog; 6. young; 7. right; 8. section; 9. four; 10. beautiful; 11. designed; 12. stained

Page 55
1–5. Answers will vary but should convey the appropriate emotion.
6. S, P; 7. P, S; 8. S, P; 9. P, S; 10. S, S

Page 56
1. ?; 2. ?; 3. ?; 4. !; 5. !; 6. ?; 7. !; 8. ?; 9. You will not believe this!
10. What are you talking about?

Answer Key

11. Wow! A snail has teeth on its tongue! 12. Goodness! There are thousands of tiny teeth!

Page 57
Answers will vary but should resemble:
1. highly ranked; 2. worthy of respect; 3. beat, conquered; 4. power, authority; 5. like a king; 6. occupied a place; 7. stories that have been passed down

Page 58
1. D, f; 2. J, a; 3. K, b; 4. I, g; 5. E, d; 6. G or L, e; 7. B, k; 8. A, h; 9. H, j; 10. C, c; 11. F, l; 12. G or L, i

Page 59
1–10. Answers will vary.

Page 60
Answers will vary but may include 1. easy to do; 2. speechless, can't find the right words; 3. old; far along in life; 4. go to bed; 5. ready to listen; 6–10. Answers will vary.

Page 61
1. M; 2. S; 3. S; 4. M; 5. S;
6–7. Answers will vary but must include either a metaphor or a simile. 8. B; 9. A; 10. A

Page 62
1. old; 2. hot; 3. dirty; 4. win; 5. catch; 6. fast; 7. humble; 8. sloppy; 9. pretty; 10. quiet; 11. small; 12. intelligent; 13. old; 14. party; 15. tired; 16. hard

Page 63
1–5. Answers will vary.

Page 68
1. 42 is 6 times as many as 7. 42 is 7 times as many as 6. 2. 8 is 2 times as many as 4. 8 is 4 times as many as 2. 3. 40 is 5 times as many as 8. 40 is 8 times as many as 5. 4. 21 is 3 times as many as 7. 21 is 7 times as many as 3. 5. 36 is 4 times as many as 9. 36 is 9 times as many as 4. 6. 72 is 6 times as many as 12. 72 is 12 times as many as 6. 7. 27 is 3 times

as many as 9. 27 is 9 times as many as 3. 8. 20 is 4 times as many as 5. 20 is 5 times as many as 4.

Page 69
1. 6 x 8 = 48; 2. 7 x 4 = 28; 3. 12 x 7 = 84; 4. 5 x 11 = 55; 5. 6 x 9 = 54; 6. 9 x 8 = 72; 7. 9 x 3 = 27; 8. 7 x 9 = 63

Page 70
1. 5, 5; 2. 8, 3; 3. 10, 8; 4. $15, 3, $5

Page 71
2. 5 × 6 = 30 cards; 3. 16 ÷ 2 = 8 pairs of shoes; 4. 8 × 4 = 32 coins; 5. 21 ÷ 3 = 7 rocks

Page 72
Elizabeth, 82; Jacob, 73; Eric, 72; George, 8; Emily, 77; Claire, 24; Demetri, 48

Page 73
1. 6 crayons; 2. $7; 3. 70 books; 4. 3 jelly beans

Page 74
1. 1, 2, 4, 7, 8, 14, 28, 56; 2. 1, 3, 9, 11, 33, 99; 3. 1, 2, 3, 4, 6, 8, 9, 12, 18, 24, 36, 72; 4. 1, 2, 5, 10, 25, 50

Page 75
1. 4; 2. 6; 3. 16; 4. 21; 5. 7; 6. 5; 7. 7; 8. 20; 9. 3; 10. 9; 11. 1, 2, 3, 5, 6, 10, 15, 30; 12. 1, 5, 25; 13. 1, 2, 4, 8, 10, 20, 40; 14. 1, 2, 4, 8, 16, 32

Page 76
Answers will vary.

Page 77
1. 29, 37, 46; Rule: +1, +2, +3…; 2. 46, 41, 36; Rule: −5; 3. 16, 16, 32; Rule: × 1, × 2; 4. 236, 246, 492; Rule × 2, +10; 5. 79, 72, 64; Rule: −1, −2, −3…; 6. 50, 53, 106; Rule: +3, × 2; 7. 19, 25, 24; Rule: −1, +6; 8. 339, 329, 987; Rule: × 3, −10; 9. $\frac{5}{4}, \frac{11}{8}, \frac{3}{2}$; Rule: + $\frac{1}{8}$; 10. 64, 640, 128; Rule ÷5, × 10

Page 78
1. 70 + 7; 2. 300 + 50 + 7; 3. 2,000 + 500 +

Answer Key

60; **4.** 400 + 50 + 9; **5.** 3,000 + 900 + 10 + 2; **6.** 1000 + 3; **7.** 80 + 8, 80 is ten times 8; 8. 500 + 50 + 5, 500 is ten times 50, which is ten times 5; 9. 30 + 3, 30 is ten times 3; 10. 200 + 20 + 2, 200 is ten times 20, which is ten times 2

Page 79
1. <; 2. =; 3. <; 4. >; 5. <; 6. <; 7. >; 8. <; 9. >; 10. =; 11. <; 12. <; 13. 1,400,892, 1,408,241, 9,426,597; 14. 328,191, 340,384, 342,192; 15. 65,382, 68,297, 405,495 929,058; 16. 385,722, 395,024, 409,990, 456,817

Page 80
1. $700; 2. $100; 3. $600; 4. $3,700; 5. $1,700; 6. $900; 7. $1,456,800; 8. $345,200; 9. $250,000

Page 81
1. 70; 2. 60; 3. 10; 4. 60; 5. 80; 6. 20; 7. 50; 8. 30; 9. 300; 10. 900; 11. 600; 12. 400; 13. 800; 14. 700; 15. 700; 16. 200; 17. 1,000; 18. 2,000; 19. 1,000; 20. 4,000; 21. 6,000; 22. 8,000; 23. 10,000; 24. 4,000; 25. 6,000; 26. 20,000; 27. 100,000; 28. 10,000; 29. 200,000; 30. 1,000,000; 31. 200,000

Page 82
1. 595; 2. 606; 3. 416; 4. 3,934; 5. 7,505; 6. 4,895; 7. 8,258; 8. 5,736; 9. 6,338; 10. 35,298; 11. 177; 12. 158; 13. 146; 14. 466; 15. 19,287; 16. 495; 17. 828; 18. 395; 19. 1,389; 20. 14,538; 21. 412; 22. 172; 23. 183; 24. 346; 25. 221

Page 83
1. 434 black ants; 2. 1,292 pounds; 3. 553 feet; 4. 1,078 butterflies; 5. 46,084 insects; 6. 10,176 birds; 7. 1,785 insects; 8. 957 monarch butterflies

Page 84
1. 105; 2. 96; 3. 88; 4. 82; 5. 26; 6. 68; 7. 38; 8. 72; 9. 70; 10. 94; 11. 144; 12. 108; 13. 216; 14. 162; 15. 114; 16. 581; 17. 152; 18. 260; 19. 738; 20. 371; 21. 194; 22. 196; 23. 232; 24. 380; 25. 465; 26. 444; 27. 595; 28. 177; 29. 372; 30. 188; 31. 462; 32. 366; 33. 644; 34. 840; 35. 824; 36. 360; 37. 354; 38. 436; 39. 916; 40. 814; 41. 705; 42. 692; 43. 368; 44. 984; 45. 1,168; 46. 706; 47. 1,524;

48. 1,386

Page 85
1. 74; 2. 444; 3. 256; 4. 2,176; 5. 72; 6. 1,992; 7. 312; 8. 768; 9. 264; 10. 414; 11. 1,768; 12. 1,032; 13. 408; 14. 1,271; 15. 345; 16. 714; 17. 689; 18. 204; 19. 1,302; 20. 350; 21. 800; 22. 357; 23. 385; 24. 338; 25. 870; 26. 1,088; 27. 4,200; 28. 1,005; 29. 2,173; 30. 1,197

Page 86
1. 703 people; 2. 336 people; 3. 570 minutes; 4. 360 seeds; 5. 5,922 square feet; 6. 150,000 sheets; 7. 1,380 ants

Page 87
1. 19; 2. 30r1; 3. 17r1; 4. 8r2; 5. 17r1; 6. 12r1; 7. 24r1; 8. 8r2; 9. 5r3; 10. 15r4; 11. 78; 12. 84r2; 13. 165r2; 14. 101r2; 15. 338r1; 16. 92r5; 17. 108r1; 18. 47; 19. 203r1; 20. 27; 21. 92; 22. 91; 23. 27; 24. 63; 25. 67r1

Page 88
1. 82r5; 2. 64; 3. 51r2; 4. 46r4; 5. 113; 6. 503r1; 7. 2,812r1; 8. 692; 9. 1,022r3; 10. 441r3; 11. 564r6; 12. 936r2; 13. 1895r4; 14. 2,118; 15. 2,293; 16. 3,335r1; 17. 856; 18. 432; 19. 1,893r1; 20. 439r1

Page 89
1. 215 cartons; 2. 801 boxes; 3. 1,330 packages, 5 seeds left over; 4. 811 bottles; 5. 48 boxes; 6. 405 vases, 2 flowers left over; 7. 398 bottles; 8. 306 packages, 1 piece left over

Page 90
1. $\frac{2}{6} = \frac{1}{3}$; 2. $\frac{1}{4} = \frac{2}{8}$; 3. $\frac{1}{2} = \frac{3}{6}$; 4. $\frac{3}{4} = \frac{6}{8}$;

5. $\frac{2}{2} = 1$; 6. $\frac{3}{7} = \frac{6}{14}$; 7. $\frac{1}{5} = \frac{2}{10}$; 8. $\frac{1}{6} = \frac{2}{12}$;

9. $\frac{8}{8} = 1$; 10. $\frac{1}{3} = \frac{3}{9}$; 11. $\frac{2}{4} = \frac{8}{16}$; 12. $\frac{1}{4} = \frac{3}{12}$

Page 91
1. $\frac{4}{8}$; 2. $\frac{3}{6}$; 3. $\frac{2}{6}$; 4. $\frac{8}{16}$; 5. 12; 6. 3; 7. 10; 8. 12; 9. 1; 10. 6

Answer Key

Page 92

1. $\frac{40}{100} + \frac{8}{100} = \frac{48}{100}$; 2. $\frac{3}{100} + \frac{70}{100} = \frac{73}{100}$; 3. $\frac{1}{100} + \frac{90}{100} = \frac{91}{100}$; 4. $\frac{30}{100} + \frac{7}{100} = \frac{37}{100}$; 5. $\frac{9}{100} + \frac{90}{100} = \frac{99}{100}$; 6. $\frac{110}{100} + \frac{11}{100} = \frac{121}{100}$; 7. $\frac{2}{100} + \frac{30}{100} = \frac{32}{100}$; 8. $\frac{50}{100} + \frac{7}{100} = \frac{57}{100}$; 9. $\frac{20}{100} + \frac{3}{100} + \frac{10}{100} = \frac{33}{100}$; 10. $\frac{50}{100} + \frac{7}{100} + \frac{5}{100} = \frac{62}{100}$

Page 93

1. $\frac{1}{3} < \frac{2}{3}$; 2. $\frac{1}{4} = \frac{2}{8}$; 3. $\frac{3}{8} < \frac{1}{2}$; 4. $\frac{1}{3} = \frac{2}{6}$; 5. $\frac{3}{4} > \frac{2}{4}$; 6. $\frac{1}{2} = \frac{2}{4}$

Page 94

1. >; 2. >; 3. >; 4. =; 5. >; 6. <; 7. >; 8. >; 9. <; 10. =; 11. =; 12. <; 13. <; 14. <; 15. = 16. <

Page 95

1. $\frac{3}{4}$; 2. $\frac{1}{4}$; 3. $\frac{4}{5}$; 4. $\frac{9}{10}$; 5. $\frac{1}{4}$; 6. $\frac{3}{5}$; 7. $\frac{8}{9}$; 8. $\frac{1}{3}$; 9. $\frac{2}{5}$; 10. $\frac{4}{5}$; 11. $\frac{2}{5}$; 12. $\frac{1}{5}$

Page 96

1. $\frac{1}{6}$; 2. $\frac{4}{4}$ or 1; 3. $\frac{1}{8}$; 4. $\frac{24}{12}$ or 2; 5. $\frac{5}{5}$ or 1; 6. $\frac{11}{8}$ or 1 $\frac{3}{8}$; 7. $\frac{11}{11}$ or 1; 8. $\frac{9}{7}$ or 1 $\frac{2}{7}$; 9. $\frac{3}{5}$; 10. $\frac{10}{9}$ or 1 $\frac{1}{9}$; 11. $\frac{1}{2}$; 12. $\frac{17}{13}$ or 1 $\frac{4}{13}$

Page 97

1. $\frac{6}{8}$ or $\frac{3}{4}$ mile; 2. Answers may vary but may include that it is $\frac{4}{8}$, or half of the race. 3. $\frac{3}{8}$, sprint; 4. Answers will vary. 5. Answers will vary.

Page 98

1. $\frac{2}{2}$ or 1; 2. $\frac{11}{6}$ or 1 $\frac{5}{6}$; 3. $\frac{6}{5}$ or 1 $\frac{1}{5}$; 4. $\frac{7}{3}$ or 2 $\frac{1}{3}$; 5. $\frac{11}{4}$ or 2 $\frac{3}{4}$; 6. $\frac{17}{6}$ or 2 $\frac{5}{6}$

Page 99

1. 4 $\frac{4}{5}$; 2. 9 $\frac{4}{5}$; 3. 9 $\frac{9}{14}$; 4. 6 $\frac{1}{2}$; 5. 11 $\frac{5}{12}$; 6. 3 $\frac{3}{8}$; 7. 9 $\frac{2}{9}$; 8. 7 $\frac{1}{6}$; 9. 13 $\frac{2}{5}$; 10. 4 $\frac{1}{2}$; 11. 8 $\frac{2}{15}$; 12. 6 $\frac{1}{12}$

Page 100

1. 1 $\frac{5}{7}$; 2. 2 $\frac{2}{3}$; 3. $\frac{2}{6}$ or $\frac{1}{3}$; 4. 5 $\frac{6}{8}$ or 5 $\frac{3}{4}$; 5. 2 $\frac{3}{5}$; 6. $\frac{6}{10}$ or $\frac{3}{5}$; 7. 2 $\frac{3}{5}$; 8. 2 $\frac{10}{12}$ or 2 $\frac{5}{6}$; 9. $\frac{4}{8}$ or $\frac{1}{2}$; 10. $\frac{6}{9}$ or $\frac{2}{3}$; 11. 1 $\frac{10}{12}$ or 1 $\frac{5}{6}$; 12. 5 $\frac{2}{4}$ or 5 $\frac{1}{2}$

Page 101

1. 2; 2. 1 $\frac{3}{5}$; 3. $\frac{6}{7}$; 4. 1 $\frac{1}{7}$; 5. 2 $\frac{2}{5}$; 6. $\frac{9}{10}$; 7. 6 $\frac{3}{4}$; 8. 1 $\frac{4}{5}$; 9. 1 $\frac{1}{3}$; 10. 1 $\frac{5}{7}$; 11. $\frac{3}{5}$; 12. 1 $\frac{1}{2}$; 13. 1 $\frac{1}{2}$; 14. 1 $\frac{1}{9}$; 15. $\frac{6}{7}$; 16. 2 $\frac{2}{3}$

Page 102

1. 3 students; 2. 9 girls; 3. 4 students; 4. 4 students; 5. 6 students; 6. 21 students

Page 103

1. $\frac{4}{10}$, 0.4; 2. $\frac{2}{10}$, 0.2; 3. $\frac{5}{10}$, 0.5; 4. 1 $\frac{4}{10}$, 1.4; 5. 1 $\frac{1}{10}$, 1.1; 6. 1 $\frac{9}{10}$, 1.9

Page 104

1. $\frac{21}{100}$, 0.21; 2. $\frac{47}{100}$, 0.47; 3. $\frac{34}{100}$, 0.34; 4. $\frac{69}{100}$, 0.69; 5. 1 $\frac{7}{100}$, 1.07; 6. 1 $\frac{2}{100}$, 1.02

Page 105

1. 9.16; 2. 14.72; 3. 200.34; 4. 47.89; 5. 11.62; 6. $\frac{2}{25}$; 7. 6 $\frac{9}{100}$; 8. 2 $\frac{3}{25}$;

Answer Key

9. $\frac{21}{100}$; 10. $7\frac{17}{50}$; 11. $\frac{11}{20}$; 12. $16\frac{2}{25}$; 13. $300\frac{6}{25}$; 14. $25\frac{1}{25}$; 15. $600\frac{49}{100}$; 16. $\frac{18}{25}$; 17. $\frac{11}{50}$; 18. $25\frac{17}{50}$; 19. $9\frac{9}{100}$; 20. $4\frac{39}{100}$

Page 106
1. 0.5, 1.5, 2.5, 3.5; 2. 4.5, 5.5, 6.5, 7.5; 3. 0.5, 1, 1.5, 2; 4. 1.5, 2, 2.5, 3; 5. 0.5, 2.5, 3, 3.5; 6. 2.5, 3.5, 4, 4.5, 5.5

Page 107
1. >; 2. <; 3. >; 4. <; 5. <; 6. <; 7. >; 8. >; 9. >; 10. >; 11. <; 12. >; 13. <; 14. <; 15. <

Page 108
1. 3,000; 2. 8; 3. 14; 4. 84; 5. 9,000; 6. 41; 7. 73,000; 8. 57; 9. 25; 10. 7; 11. 12,000; 12. 118; 13. 6; 14. 2; 15. 65,000; 16. 4 grams; 17. 15,000 milligrams; 18. 2,000 grams; 19. 16 grams

Page 109
1. 8,000; 2. 5; 3. 15,000; 4. 48; 5. 4,000; 6. 33; 7. 92,000; 8. 21,000; 9. 7; 10. 6,000; 11. 8; 12. 27,000; 13. 18 liters; 14. 500 milliliters; 15. 14,000 milliliters; 16. 12 liters, 6 bottles

Page 110
1. 8:45; 2. 10:15; 3. 8:15; 4. 10:45; 5. 10:45; 6. 11:45; 7. 12:00; 8. 1:45; 9. 2:20 pm; 10. 9:55 pm; 11. 7:30 am; 12. 10:00 pm

Page 111
1. $14.83; 2. $5.75; 3. $5.47; 4. $32.00; 5. $20.25; 6. $4.67

Page 112
1. 24 feet; 2. 35 centimeters; 3. 280 meters; 4. 310 inches; 5. 120 inches; 6. 336 inches; 7. 146 feet; 8. 55 inches

Page 113
1. 28 square inches; 2. 64 square meters; 3. 80 square meters; 4. 25 square centimeters; 5. 420 square inches; 6. 975 square inches; 7. 54 square yards; 8. 495 square feet

Page 114
1. $\frac{4}{8}$ or $\frac{1}{2}$ inch; 2. $\frac{1}{2}$ inch; 3. place dot over $\frac{3}{4}$; 4. $\frac{5}{8}$ inch

Page 115
1. acute; 2. right; 3. obtuse; 4. right; 5. obtuse; 6. acute; 7. obtuse; 8. right

Page 116
1. 62°, acute; 2. 153°, obtuse; 3. 30°, acute; 4. 14°, acute; 5. 123°, obtuse; 6. 90°, right; 7. 45°, acute; 8. 112°, obtuse; 9. 136°, obtuse; 10-12. Check child's work.

Page 117
1. 60; 2. 75; 3. 1; 4. 20; 5. 61; 6. 55; 7. 45; 8. 38

Page 118
1. ray CD; 2. line CM; 3. line segment XY; 4. line AB; 5. line segment BC; 6. line ST; 7. intersecting; 8. parallel; 9. perpendicular

Page 119
Check child's work. 1–6. Lines should not touch. 7–12. Lines should form right angles.

Page 120
1. equilateral; 2. isosceles; 3. scalene; 4. scalene; 5. scalene; 6. equilateral; 7. right; 8. obtuse; 9. acute; 10. obtuse; 11. right; 12. acute

Page 121
1. yes; 2. yes; 3. yes; 4. no; 5. yes; 6. yes; 7. no; 8. no; 9. yes; 10. no; 11. yes; 12. yes; 13. yes; 14. yes; 15. no;

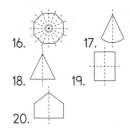

16. 17. 18. 19. 20.